SECRETS OF AN AD PRO

SECRETS OF AN AD PRO

A money-making guide to creating great advertising and living the good life...without selling your soul

George A. Scott

WRITERS CLUB PRESS
SAN JOSE NEW YORK LINCOLN SHANGHAI

Secrets of an Ad Pro
A money-making guide to creating great advertising and
living the good life...without selling your soul

Writers Club Press
an imprint of iUniverse.com, Inc.

For information address:
iUniverse.com, Inc.
5220 S 16th, Ste. 200
Lincoln, NE 68512
www.iuniverse.com

ISBN: 0-595-19419-2

Printed in the United States of America

Epigraph

"This above all...to thine own self be true and it must follow as the night the day thou canst not then be false to any man." Act 1, Scene 3 from Hamlet by William Shakespeare, the greatest copywriter of them all

Contents

Acknowledgements

IN APPRECIATION
To Michel Martin, my office manager, proofreader
and loving daughter;
to Jil Scott, my wife, partner and cheerleader for half a century;
to Jim Stano (Jim Words), Jim Taliana (Jim Pix),
Fred Simper (part-time Fred),
Doug Powers (the street-fighter) as well as Jack Carmichael,
Claudia Stroud, Bob Ryeson,
Paul Stawski, Gary Slomka, Dick Wolf and all the other
members of my Cadillac creative team at DMB&B
during the glory days;
to Chuck Adams, Ernie Jones, Pete Moore, Dick Monley,
Jim Doyle, Ron Monchak and all the other members of
DMB&B management;
to the cofounder (with myself) of Greenhouse, my focus-group
traveling companion,
DMB&B marketing guru and friend Lu DiSalvo;
to Ralph Gardella who has made my years heading up Encore
North & South
since retiring from DMB&B so enjoyable;
A special note of appreciation to
Jack Taylor, Margie Gobler, John Taylor, Lori Taylor,
Becky Wyble
and all the other members of TEAM STI for making
these last dozen years
of my career so rewarding

Introduction

Maybe you don't know me. That's okay I probably don't know you either. But let me tell you where I'm coming from.

Even at the beginning of my career in advertising, it was never my intent to win fame and fortune. Only to live the good life. And that I have done for more than 35 years…and am doing now running my own business in semi-retirement.

All thanks to advertising. The field has been good to me…and, in all humility, I to it.

Someone (maybe it was me) once wisely said: "The only true wealth is the freedom to do what you want to do when you want to do it." By that standard, I am a wealthy man. (And a lot of rich people are not.) As "snow birds", my wife Jil and I alternate between our home in Fort Myers, Florida for the winter and a cottage on a lake in Michigan for the summer. We go where we want, do what we want and truly enjoy life. The last thing we worry about is money.

If that kind of wealth appeals to you, I can help you attain it. By revealing a goodly number of creative secrets not available in ad school—or anywhere else for that matter. Not that I'm knocking formal education in our many fine colleges and universities. Far from it because I have taught courses in both advertising and marketing at two very good universities. It's just that I'm in a position to tell you things they can't tell you. Things I have learned the hard way from sometimes bitter experience while working for a big-time agency doing battle for major league accounts…and since retirement running my own shop in Michigan and Florida.

One last thing and for me it's the most important of all and the stated purpose of this book. You don't have to cheat…lie…step on people…step over people to succeed. I like to think I am living proof you can make it big in advertising without being an SOB.

Here's how.

CHAPTER ONE

The Business

Granted. I have met my share of jerks, creeps, bastards and SOBs in this select community we call the advertising business. Most are harmless enough. (We'll talk later about how to handle the few deadly ones.)

But the truly surprising thing is that the public's conception of the men and women who people this business is 180 off. At least from my point of view, based upon a lifetime of playing creative hardball in the big leagues of ad biz.

Better than 85 percent of the people I have worked with and for are decent people. And I use that word very carefully. Decent. It doesn't mean that many are not shortsighted sometimes…self-centered (who isn't?)…and plagued by the human vices we love appealing to in advertising. Like greed, lust and power. Yes, they may be tainted a bit.

But, God love them, they are decent. With good hearts…a sense of right and wrong…and, most important, the ability to laugh at themselves. I am totally convinced the level of decency in this business equals or exceeds that of almost any other. Including, physicians, lawyers and positively politicians.

Why this is so puzzles me.

Here is a business held in low esteem and yet it seems to attract and keep an astonishing high number of talented, charming and, yes, decent people. It might be that the work is interesting, challenging and well-paid. Another reason might be that "it ain't brain surgery". People in it believe in this business and the way things should be done. But not so much that they're going to kill somebody for their beliefs. We take what we do seriously. But most of us don't take ourselves seriously.

I suspect many people in the business look at it the way I do. I work like hell. Fight like hell to win. But deep down inside I know it is a game. A game more interesting than Monopoly or Bridge. And the beautiful part is you get paid for playing it.

Inside this business, you will find a high level of pride. Nobody I know who has done well has the least sense of shame. Quite the opposite. I have found if you believe in yourself and what you are doing, it shines through. People will believe in you. Including client people. More than 90 percent of the client people I have served have been lovely people. Tough, as they should be. But responsive, fair and yes again, decent.

What happens when you come up against a client who isn't decent? What if he is one of the deadly ones—a dyed in-the-wool son-of-a-bitch. It happened to me when I was a vp, copy/contact guy for a grand old San Diego agency called Barnes/Chase Advertising. I should have suspected something. It was a large, new real estate development just north of San Diego with lakes, streams, a golf course, private homes and condos. Quite attractive. I made the pitch to the three brothers who owned and operated it. When I finished with a bit of a flourish, there was nothing but silence. The two younger brothers looked for direction from oldest brother.

He said nothing for what seemed an eternity.

"We'll let you know," was finally his only response.

All of us were surprised and pleased when oldest brother called a week later to say we had the account. We shouldn't have been pleased. Oldest brother rapidly began a campaign to make my life miserable. Nothing we did was good enough for him. And yet, he would give us no direction. He dominated and mentally abused his younger brothers in our presence. And worst of all, he was totally devoid of a sense of humor.

As leader of the agency/creative team, I tried to cope. Week by week, the situation became more intolerable. Finally, I took action—or ran away—depending upon your point of view. I informed the client and agency management that I had to take a week of my vacation right now. My wife Jil and I just took off in the car and headed for the High Sierras.

A week later, we returned and I had made my decision. In a meeting with our management, I made it clear I could not and would not work with oldest brother. In a very real sense, I put my job on the line. They said they understood completely. The account was reassigned to another poor devil and in three weeks we lost the business.

If this kind of thing happens to you, there are a limited number of actions open to you.

They are:

1. Endure it.
2. Try to change it.
3. Kill the bastard.
4. Escape from it.

In my opinion, number one if out of the question as a permanent solution.

An art director I once worked with put it beautifully:

"Life is too short to deal with pricks."

Take your choice of the other three. But do not—I repeat do not—learn to live with it. You're too good for that.

CHAPTER TWO

The System

I admit it. I hate systems.

Always have. In my opinion, systems are an emotional crutch for the insecure. Too often, following a system is a poor substitute for creating solutions to problems. While systems proponents claim they free the mind to concentrate on the vital, I am convinced they do the opposite. Systems may lead to efficiency but I have never seen them alone result in great advertising. Never.

But.

But I have developed a simple system that works every time. If you combine it with hard work and brilliance. Yet, you say, any system will succeed with those two ingredients. Wrong.

Before I reveal my system…a warning. Like all big and successful ideas, it will appear to be "just good common sense". Or, it might seem obvious to you. Wrong again. If you want to make successful creative presentations every time…live the good life…and retire to Florida early to dwell in comfort and luxury…pay attention!

My system has only three basic parts. Three is just right—not too few…not too many. Each of these parts has three parts. And you can continue that basic division by three if it pleases you.

The three basics are:

1. Develop a communication plan.
2. Create the creative.
3. Sell the program.

Before we discuss each part, stop a minute. Consider the obvious. You can't create advertising until you have a plan. But many big time ad people try. And small timers too. The insidious thing about this business is it appears so damn simple to some and so damn complex to others. The truth is it is not as simple as outsiders would have it. Yet, it is no way as complex as the eggheads perceive it to be in their printed monuments to analysis paralysis.

Part 1. Develop a communication plan.
And how do you do this? It's the same basic procedure for all kinds of clients—big or small...consumer, industrial, retail. It doesn't matter. You start at the beginning with...

Step 1. Situation Analysis.
In plain English, where do we stand? What are we trying to sell—in both physical and emotional terms? What is the product or service and what does it do for people? Next, what is the economic climate? Examine the competitive environment. Consumer attitudes toward our product and theirs. Awareness of our product. Channels of distribution. Dealer attitudes (distributor, whatever). Pricing policy. Packaging.

Overall, what are our problems and opportunities? What are our strengths and our weaknesses? Of course, we'll want to correct or circumvent our weaknesses. (Getting the client to correct even an obvious weakness is often difficult for the agency.) Most of all, we're going to accentuate our strengths in our plan.

As you begin to get answers to your questions, write them down. Surprisingly, most of the information you seek is readily available. From the client or prospect, from annual reports (which even the client doesn't read carefully), trade journals, from trade/business associations and most of all on the Net. Sometimes even the government can be helpful. The gold is there for those who will but dig.

Time and again I have delighted the client with the depth and breadth of information we had gleaned from his own organization or his publications.

Step 2. Marketing Objectives/Strategies.

Where do we want to be…how do we get there? Step 1 was the digging part and now we're going to put this knowledge together in a meaningful way and do something with it.

First off, we want to develop a written mission statement. I repeat: A written mission statement. Nothing you can do for and with the client is more important than this. Nothing.

Time and again I have seen the fortunes of major companies turned around by successful completion of this one vital step. Once everybody agrees on what they're trying to accomplish, everything else seems to fall into place.

Example: Pontiac. During the 1970s this once proud nameplate fell on hard times. Our agency had served both Pontiac and Cadillac since the 1930s but somehow Pontiac (and the agency team) had lost the way. No one knew what the role of Pontiac was or should be in the marketplace.

Finally, wiser heads prevailed. The client and the agency in a long and tedious effort hammered out a mission statement together. It was clear. Concise. Simple. And most of all, it was single-minded. The essence of the mission of the Division could be summarized by a single word.

Excitement.

And, as they say, the rest is history. To the tune of "Pontiac builds excitement", the agency (now DMB&B) created great advertising built eventually around a whole new series of exciting cars. Including the Trans Am, the Firebird and the Grand Am.

After completion of the written mission statement, work can proceed on the rest of Step 2. Of course, each becomes a part of your written communications plan and the basics for our presentation to the client or prospect. They are:

. Development of short-term communications objectives and resulting strategies.

. Long-term communications objectives and strategies.

. Development of a clear, simple premise or promise for the advertising. The simpler the better

In plain English, what does the product or service offer the consumer?

. Based upon this premise, the mission statement and all you know, develop a communications strategy in outline form. What now is your master plan? State it clearly and concisely.

. Lastly in Step 2, indicate a direction for your creative strategy. Chances are, it's too early in the game to carry this very far. But no doubt some things now seem obvious. State them to both impress the client/ prospect with your clear thinking and to lay the groundwork for what lies ahead.

Step 3. Specific Recommendations.

As all other elements in your communications plan, your specific recommendations should be written in outline form for your formal presentation to the client/prospect and become a part of the leave-behind.

Most important, all your recommendations should carry an estimated price tag and be based upon those clearly stated communications objectives you have developed.

Elements to include are:

. **Creative execution**. We're not talking about specific ads or commercials at this point but rather overall direction that will affect cost. Are you considering the use of a celebrity...a TV spectacular? Or the opposite...small-space newspaper or local radio? Talk about it in outline form and estimate its costs.

. **Media plan**. Here you can become more specific. We have found it most effective to offer a choice of plans—usually three. (1) A bare-bones minimum effort. (2) A more effective plan costing more. (3) A program that would be the most cost efficient. Be sure to make provision for print advertising or broadcast production. Depending upon the budget, a good rule of thumb is 15 to 20 percent of total media costs.

. **Collateral support.** What is needed in the way of sales literature, dealer support materials, you name it? And, of course, how much do you or your agency want to become involved? It's your decision, but I have found that the agency that does the advertising is best equipped to do the collateral. It can work to the advantage of both agency and client. Again, be specific. State and describe each piece of collateral, what it will involve in content and quantity and a cost estimate, as well as an estimate of production time.

. **The Internet.** You'll find a wide range of opinions as to its effectiveness right now as an advertising vehicle but one thing is clear. Your client should be on it. On the positive side, costs are low and the potential is tremendous. A second point is clear…find somebody who has a proven record of success advertising on the web to work with you unless you really know what you are doing. Thirdly, use the special magic of the web but never let it get in the way of your basic message.

. **PR help**. As important as it is, advertising is but one weapon in the communications arsenal. Public relations in the form of publicity, trade shows and other efforts to involve the media can be tremendously important and effective. Whether you or your agency handle it, you should state the need if it exists and what you estimate it will cost.

. **Marketing research**. Are there holes in your quest for information that require research before a communications plan can be finalized? Are there key questions that must be answered about consumer attitudes relating to this product or service? To discover in real-world terms just how effective this advertising is going to be, it may be advisable to establish tracking studies before, during and after the advertising program runs. State what this research will accomplish, what it will involve, what it will cost and how long it will take.

These then are the three steps in developing a communications plan (Part 1 of Scott's Simple System). I suggest you follow all the written outline elements with summary budget sheets that show all elements of the plan, costs of each and a total figure. Again, no one is thrilled about being boxed in. We have found the modular approach that gives a client or prospect a little choice is most effective. Three is the magic number. Give them a good, better and best. Plan A. Plan B. Plan C.

One last point about the communications plan. For God's sake, don't give it away. The best thinking of your best people should go into its development so you should get all or a portion of its cost back. Charging for it also solicits a commitment from the client or prospect. As well as: "How good can it be, if it's for free?"

Okay, I know what you're thinking at this point. "For a guy who hates systems, he's sure sounding like he's hooked on one." Not really. Go back over what we've covered so far. I think you'll agree what I'm presenting to you is no more than a simple, clear roadmap. So you won't end up in Cleveland when you wanted to go to L.A. It's frightening easy to do that in this business. I've seen it happen many times. Hell, I've helped make it happen…earlier in my career. More times than I like to think about.

Next, the fun part.

CHAPTER THREE

The Creative

The angle.

The creative inspiration.

The big idea.

Whatever you call it, the key question is: How do you get it? Introducing the second part of your quest toward great advertising…"Creating the creative". I have the system that's sure to work for you—if you have the talent and determination. But first, let's shoot down a few myths that have made a few pseudo-intellectuals big bucks.

One is what I call the "Black Magic Theory". It alleges that ad people are possessed with strange and unnatural powers to influence the gullible American public any way they wish. Working behind the scenes with devious devices, they can get anybody to buy almost anything.

This is, of course, pure crap.

Sorry, Vance, these hidden persuaders do not exist. Never have. Never will. For one simple reason. The much-maligned American consumer is one smart cookie. You don't fool her or him for long. If you don't believe that, consider this. I have worked in advertising practically all my long adult life. I have worked in the minor leagues and the big leagues—on some of the biggest and best-known names in American business—and have gotten to know many of the giants in the industry. If these Black

Magic methods existed, I would have damn well run across them. And tried them.

Dear friend, there is only one way on God's earth that you can influence anybody to do anything. I humbly call it Scott's law:

THE ONLY WAY TO GET ANYBODY TO DO ANYTHING IS THROUGH HIS OR HER OWN SELF-INTEREST.

That's it! That's where the magic is. In creating fresh, new ways to do this better than your competitors. And that leads to a definition of creative advertising that settles all the arguments.

CREATIVE ADVERTISING IS ADVERTISING THAT WORKS.

The role of advertising isn't to make you laugh or cry. It's to make you buy. Okay. So how do we do that? How do we create great advertising by appealing to would-be buyers through their own self-interest?

It isn't easy. But it can be done—if you follow the system. And use that God-given talent that most of us have hidden away. Plus, patience and perseverance.

Part Two..."Creating the Creative"...has six steps. Hold it! I know six is not three. I'm sorry. There is just no way it can be done in only three. In the advertising game you have to learn to be flexible.

The six steps are:

1. Absorb.
2. Create consciously.
3. Switch brains.
4. Ah ha!
5. Expand it.
6. Test it.

They're easy to learn and simple to apply. Let's discuss each.

Step 1...Absorb. You've come a long way...having completed development of your communications plan. In the process, you decided upon your long-term and short-term objectives, as well as a clear, simple premise, a communication strategy and a creative strategy.

Now you're ready to put them into action. Step 1 is indeed **absorb**…meaning that you seek to soak up everything that relates in any way to the marketing of your product or service. This will include everything you learned in developing your communications plan and more. At all times, however, your emphasis should be from the consumer's point of view.

Your mind will be buzzing with a thousand and one details as you absorb the environment that is relevant to the product. You must literally become the consumer-with his or her thoughts…desires…prejudices…and dreams.

If you are truly meant for this business, you can do it and have fun in the process. Listen to everything the client has to say and show, of course. But, more important, get inside that consumer's brain. So much so that you **are** the consumer. You think and act like the consumer.

Step 2…Create consciously. You are now ready to begin to create conscious solutions for your marketing/advertising challenge.

For a number of years, a debate has raged over the right brain/left brain theory. I don't propose to continue the battle here. But I have to tell you, as a guy who has sold hundreds of millions of dollars worth of goods through advertising, there is something to it. Certain facts are undeniable.

The human brain is truly divided into two parts…left and right. The left half is more concerned with the factual and the analytical…the right with feelings and emotions. The human brain does operate in both a conscious and sub-conscious state. As so many other things in life, it takes two to tango. It takes both sides of the brain…left and right…analytical and emotional…conscious and sub-conscious.

I'm making a big deal of this because I'm convinced most of us allow the left (analytical) brain to dominate the right (emotional) brain. Hell, we're instructed to do so from Grade One on. "One plus one equals two," and that's it!

Not necessarily so. Depending upon your environment or your point of view. 1 + 1 can be 11. Or ten (X). Or set at angles…five (V). Or something else again in computer language. We could kick this around for hours. But now you're going to put your left-brain to work.

Do it any way you like. I prefer secluding myself is a reasonably pleas-ant setting. My tools are primitive. It used to be my beat-up old Royal typewriter, now a computer, maybe a couple of magic markers and a ball-point pen. Plus a good supply of paper. The important thing is to begin. I like to start with copywriter rough layouts of print ad ideas, using a magic marker. The elements are a visual indication (however crude)...head-line...lines for copy block. The magic marker forces you to think big...clear...simple.

Let it rip. Paper is cheap. One idea sparks another. And another.

Then when that process begins to wear thin, I switch to the computer or the ballpoint. Again, try not to be the least bit selective at this point. Let the ideas flow. Set a time limit on this step of trying to come up with "conscious" solutions. A day. Two or three. It's your choice.

Periodically review what you've got. Does something seem to have promise? Good. Nothing does? That's okay. Not to worry at this point. When you reach your preset time limit, you must do a most difficult thing. You have to stop. That's right. Stop. Completely.

Step 3...Switch brains. Now you're going to ask your right brain to go to work for you—at a sub-conscious level. If you're anything like me, your right brain has been little more than an interested observer up to this point. That tough old left-brain won't permit it to do more.

Therefore, you have to shut down the conscious (analytical) left-brain and let the sub-conscious (emotional) right-brain take a swing at things. I literally have a short talk with my right-brain. Here's the situation, right-brain. Here's what we're trying to do, old friend. See what you can come up with. I know again what you're thinking. Baloney. Too pat. Childish.

Maybe. But it works. It has worked for me hundreds of times on hun-dreds of advertising problems. It will work for you...if you let it. After a brief chat with your sub-conscious, forget about the problem at hand and relax. Sleep. Play. Do routine chores if you must work. Don't grind your teeth. Let it happen.

Step 4…Ah ha! Some people call it the illumination stage. Some the revelation. AH HA! But, of course! Why didn't I think of it before! Suddenly, the germ of a new idea—a new creative solution—seems to come to you out of the blue. In the shower. While you're running. In a dream. Just before you go to sleep at night. In the middle of the night after you've hit the bathroom (frequent for me). As you wake up. Anywhere. Anytime.

"Of course," you find yourself saying to yourself. "It's so obvious. Why did it take me so long?" This is the power of intuition at work. Beautiful intuition that leap-frogs reason. You'll know soon enough if it's a false "ah ha". If it is, don't fight it. Let the right-brain go back to work for you.

When the real thing happens, rejoice and let it happen. Most important of all, write it down. All of it. This is priceless stuff but it can easily slip through your fingers if you're not careful. Yes, by God. It seems like a winner. Great. Go immediately to…

Step 5…Expand it. Take that precious idea of yours and use it—everywhere. TV. Print. Radio. Outdoor. Promotion. PR. Anything. Everywhere.

Nine times out of ten, if it's truly a great idea, you'll be surprised and delighted how easy it all seems now. Applications of the idea just seem to flow. One leads to another. And that to yet another. You've now forgotten all the frustration, sweat and pain that came before. Life is good. Life is sweet. You're a very clever person.

Lap it up. You've earned it.

But. It's now time to return to total reality.

Step 6…Test it. The world is full of would-be critics who would love to cripple and kill your idea. So proceed with caution. Try it first on somebody whose judgment you trust. An art director. A writer. An account person.

Be careful you pick the right person. Everyone—and I mean everyone— can criticize an idea, ad, headline, anything. It takes no skill, experience or talent to do that. It is the comfort zone for people who couldn't come up with a good creative idea if it killed them. So lacking that ability, they are quick to overlook or not even recognize the good stuff and concentrate on the negative—no matter how much of a stretch that might be. "But it won't work for women over 65 in eastern Iowa!" It doesn't matter to them that you're not trying to reach women over 65 in eastern Iowa. This person is psychologically committed to finding something negative to say. Again, ignore this person—even if it's your boss, your spouse or your otherwise best friend. Select a person whose judgment you trust and admire!

If your idea glides over this hurdle, enlist your associate's support and advice on proceeding. Ifyour gut tells you this idea of yours is right, fight for it to the death. To do that effectively, you'll have to put together a presentation package.

I prefer a flip-chart. It's easy to prepare, cheap and very effective when done right. Assume nothing. In quick and interesting fashion, cover the entire marketing/advertising challenge and how this great idea of yours solves the problem. Show how well and how easily it can be extended into all media. Be specific and professional. Then rehearse. And rehearse. And rehearse.

Still love it? Still think you're absolutely right? Good. You're ready for the meat grinder.

Every agency has one…some power structure that reviews and disapproves new ideas. I say disapproves because that's what happens most of the time. But you're ready for them.

You did it! The power structure approved your idea for further testing…in the real world of clients and consumers. First, probably with qualitative research such as focus groups and then with quantitative research where numbers can be projected for various target marketing groups and geographical areas.

It's a long and costly process, but if that idea of yours is really right, the chances are exceedingly good you're going to win.

Especially if you know how to sell yourself and your ideas…

CHAPTER FOUR

The Big Sell

Congratulations. You've developed a damn good communications plan. And with a little luck and a lot of perseverance, you have created the creative. The vital third leg of our great advertising stool is…sell the program. And in the process, sell yourself…your team…your agency…your way of doing business…and the advertising business itself. That sounds like a tall order. It is. But, if you have the talent and the guts to make it in this business, you can do it.

Again, I am living proof. I used to be a terrible presenter…a terrible salesman. As I look back at my early days in copy/contact, I hadn't progressed much from the approach I used when selling magazines as a boy.

Knock on door. Door opens. Lady of the house says: "Yes, young man?"

"You wouldn't want to buy a magazine…would you, lady?"

"No," she wouldn't. Door closes. End of pitch.

I have Norm Foster, president of Barnes Chase Advertising in San Diego at that time, for getting me started in the right direction. Norm was President of the San Diego Chamber of Commerce and an excellent presenter. I guess he saw something in me I didn't see.

He literally forced me to make a pitch for a new piece of business in the publication field. And, believe it or not, the person I was to make the pitch to was none other than another Norman—Dr. Norman Vincent Peale of Positive Thinking fame.

I dug into it with a passion. And I did something I urge you not to do. I ended up memorizing my entire presentation. Then I rehearsed it…and rehearsed it…and rehearsed it. The fateful day arrived. I made the presentation. I don't think I was that bad. Not good perhaps. But at least professional.

It was a momentous day. We didn't get the business. But I had begun the long journey toward becoming one of the better presenters in the business. (Some 28 years later my brother, Ron Scott, then president of Machining Enterprises of Detroit, had occasion to mention my initiation to Dr. Peale. He wanted to know all the details. Ron said he was enthralled by the idea he had unwittingly help launch what amounted to a new career. At age 89, he then went on to demonstrate at the church Ron attended that he had lost none of his presentation skills. Since then, Ron has gone on to attend and graduate from the seminary and found his own church in Austin, Texas with his wife Lenore, who is also an ordained minister.)

Today, I love to present. It is so damn much fun to do something you are good at and get praise for doing it. It took me many, many years of searching, plus trial and error, to become the presenter I am today.

With my help, you can do it a wee bit faster. My first bit of advice might sound like a copout. It is not. I wish to God somebody had said it to me.

Point one. LEARN FROM THE EXPERTS. In my case, that consisted of going through an intensive three-day presentation skills seminar, conducted by a New York organization and paid for by DMB&B. It was painful, eye-opening, grueling and invaluable. Two years later, I went through an updated version of the seminar.

Please try to drum up interest in such a seminar at your agency—with the agency paying the freight, of course. If this is not possible, I urge your participation in a Dale Carnegie course, a speakers bureau or the like. The important thing is to learn the basic presentation skills and to practice them until you reach a high level of professionalism and confidence. These skills include eye contact, use of the hands, voice intensity, body movement and the use of visual aids such as flip charts. (More on all this in the chapter entitled "The Pitch".)

They're all important. But even more critical is how you organize your big sell. In that, I can be of great help to you right now.

As I stated previously, the key to success with a newer account or one where multi-million bucks are involved is to use the rule of three. Don't offer the client just one creative solution to his marketing/advertising problem. Give him three. Solution A...good. Solution B...better. Solution C...best.

Solution A is the safe one. It is basically what you believe the client will find comforting. This is the one you feel confident you can sell. It gets you off on the right foot. Retailers have a saying—make a sale to begin the day...whatever you have to do. It gets you going in the right mode.

Solution B is the opposite. Here is the one that stretches the client's imagination and tolerance more than a little. It's the one you and your creative team would love to put into your portfolios. It's fresh...daring...ahead of its time.

Solution C is the perfect compromise—far and away the best of the lot. It's got it all. Daring...but not too daring. And the client is ready to love and embrace it because you've done your homework. You've showed him what he expected...what he didn't expect...and the perfect solution.

A warning. Everything you present has to be on-target and saleable—something you'd be proud to see appear on the air and in print. There can be no straw men.

Coming up with three totally saleable solutions is a tall order. Hell, creating one is tough enough. But it can be done. We (my creative team and I) did it hundreds of times at DMB&B. And my batting average in selling Solution C, good old Number 3, has to be over 800.

Sometimes the client will insist on safe Solution A. That's fine. You gave it your best shot. You took him to the top of the mountain and that's not what he wants. Solution A will work well and do a good job in the marketplace. That's victory.

Once in awhile, the client will surprise you and insist upon Solution B. Terrific. You know it will be a winner.

But mostly, the client will go along with your expert opinion and agree with you on Solution C. Beautiful. You did the work. And you had the guts to present it with conviction.

On that score…it is your job, your duty, your sacred obligation to make an agency recommendation. You do your client an injustice if you present creative material without an agency point of view and a specific recommendation for a course of action. Of course, that recommendation has been agreed to by all agency parties before the presentation. It is lunacy for agency members to disagree on creative recommendations in front of the client. (Sadly, I have seen it happen a number of times. A couple of times by top agency management. I have since labeled that: "Snatching defeat from the jaws of victory". Sad.)

What if your cup runneth over and you end up with more than three excellent solutions…four or five? That's rare but it can happen. Pick your best three. Showing more than three is dangerous. It says to the client that you agency people are unsure of yourselves.

On the other hand, what if you have only two? I suggest you work like hell until you have three. There is nothing wrong with phoning the client and telling him the truth. You have two but you want to show him three excellent creative solutions. Could you have a little more time—a week or two? It's a rare client that won't be impressed and say yes.

Another factor that is key to your success is the setup for the presentation. Assume nothing. Before showing creative work, take the client through all the steps, all the research, all the basics that led to the creative solutions you're presenting. Undoubtedly, your account team, together with your marketing/research and media people, will play key roles in this setup portion of the presentation.

Although far-reaching and extensive, this material can be handled in a crisp and interesting manner. (Please, if you can, don't let those folks put the client to sleep or worse yet get them checking their watches and twisting in their seats with boredom.) Most important, it should be single-minded and to the point. It doesn't hurt to go back over familiar ground, if it's key to the creative solution. Clients could have forgotten it or there may be new client people in attendance at this all-important session.

You have to remind yourself that, while advertising is your total focus, it is often but a small part of the weekly cares of the client people you're presenting to. Again, assume nothing.

CHAPTER FIVE

The Crutch

Once I hired a writer who had a world of talent along with one fatal flaw. He had to "do it his way". This tremendously promising person had great difficulty ever listening to advice—let alone take it. We finally came to a parting of the ways when he told me his views on research.

"I don't believe in research," he stated with more than a touch of arrogant pride. Shortly thereafter he sought and found employment elsewhere.

How in God's name can you not believe in research? It's like saying you don't believe in sunshine or rain. It exists. And thank God it does. I've heard research called nothing more than a crutch. It is most certainly that. A beautiful crutch that can be the creative person's best friend

In my view, advertising research is concerned with seeking out the attitudes, desires and motivations of the final, all-powerful judge of advertising. And that, of course, is the consumer. That's the real-world person who spends his or her own money to buy your product or that of your competitor.

I stress "real world" because the client person you are trying to convince often lives in a very special world. Take a major car account. As the client, he never has to worry about taking his car in for service…bitching like hell when service is not done right…and trying to find a ride to work.

A beautifully new, fully fueled automobile in near perfect condition is supplied to him every morning and evening. In fact, he has his choice of any model or style. And if anything ever does go wrong, no problem. It's handled with absolutely no inconvenience to our high-level automotive executive.

When it doesn't touch you personally, it's difficult to comprehend or appreciate the fury and rage that bubbles and boils over service in the real world. Yet, as a creative person trying to sell your program that will affect consumers in the real world, you must make the client begin to understand what's happening out there.

The way to do that is research. Honest research presented with total honesty. Let the consumer do the talking through such devices as video tape.

Over the years we have used focus groups effectively to do this job for us. I'm talking about well-planned and professionally executed focus groups conducted in all key areas of the country. With enough groups to cover all the kinds of people who might use your product…with the differences that exist from one geographic area to another.

We never did a focus group at DMB&B without videotaping it. At first, we worried about the effect of the taping on participants. For that reason, we often shot through one-way glass from another room and, in the process, reduced the quality of the picture. With experience, we found the taping process didn't bother participants. After five minutes, they didn't seem to notice the cameraman or equipment, even when we taped within the same room.

Three factors are key to successful focus groups. (That magic number three again.) First, you have to be sure you've recruited participants who truly represent the people you are trying to reach with your advertising. To end up with ten to twelve top people for each focus group is a difficult and demanding job. At DMB&B, we turned to the experts to do our recruiting. Our Marketing Department kept a continuing log of the top recruiters in the country—including specialists on every subject in every area.

We found the most difficult group to recruit was physicians—the easiest housewives. And they were paid accordingly. At least $100 for a doctor (max $300 to $500) while the housewife was happy to attend for a mere $25. Yet, we always enjoyed the female groups more. By their nature, men are wary creatures who are forever playing the corporate game. Women, on the other hand, are much more open and honest in their responses.

One thing you never do is mix men and women in the same group. We tried it several times and it's impossible. Especially in car groups, men seek to dominate and sadly women often let them.

Factor two is preparation. We spent as much time in preparing for a series of focus groups as we did in creating the campaign itself. In fact, it was an integral part of the creative process. As a creative director, I loved and hated focus groups. I loved them because here was a chance to "talk to the final judge". To observe the consumer firsthand. To test attitudes. To see how real people react to our creative solutions, ideas and approaches in the real world. I hated them because they required a tremendous amount of work and we knew a high percentage of that work would never make it beyond the groups.

It was my policy to observe every focus group in action. And if I couldn't make it, one of my staff would. You pick up little things attending in person that you can miss on the tape. Also, you're in position to make changes in the material on the fly.

Let me tell you there is no more humbling experience. Like it or not, these creative probes or concepts the moderator is showing are your children. And it hurts to see your children abused in your presence. It's painful to witness your precious preconceived notions being shot down in flames. Again and again.

It hurts. But it is absolutely invaluable. I was almost always convinced we had it all figured out before we went out for our focus group tour of the country. And I was almost always surprised by what happened. And when it happened again and again in group after group, we knew we were beginning to see reality. The real world in action. God bless reality.

Factor three is an excellent moderator. If you have one aboard your organization, you are fortunate. If not, it's worth the extra expense to hire a professional moderator and indoctrinate him/her well. Wise agency management will see to it that there is a continuing program in place within the agency to train moderators.

One of the best I ever saw was an agency colleague of mine...Lu DiSalvo. He headed up our Marketing Department at DMB&B/Bloomfield Hills and later joined me to head up a special unit called the Greenhouse. Lord knows, Lu had plenty to do but he seldom passed up a chance to join me for a focus group tour of the country during my 11-year stint as creative director on the Cadillac account.

It's a rare pleasure to see a real pro in action...at anything. Lu was the total professional at conducting focus groups. He worked hard at it because he loved it. Or, he loved it because he worked hard at it. Probably both.

Working as a team, he and I (and out staffs) discussed our needs at length before beginning work on the creative probes. And our discussions continued until the day we lugged the pizza bags full of foam boards out to the airport. And during the trip we conferred daily to make changes as needed and create new material if that was required.

Most of all, Lu had the magic touch in dealing with the participants. He knew when to be tough, when to be gentle, how to bring out true beliefs, attitudes and convictions of those precious consumers we were trying to influence. He loved it but it was hard work. Like a fighter going into a difficult bout, Lu would find time to take a short nap before the action. He wanted to be totally fresh and alert for the sessions themselves.

As you probably know, there are two basic kinds of research—qualitative (smaller groups for attitudes and trends) and quantitative (larger numbers of people with specifics that can be projected). We used both but I am partial to good old-fashioned focus groups when they are done right. They're relatively inexpensive, very flexible and, as a creative person, you get an opportunity to see, hear and react to your target consumer in person. He or she doesn't see you because you're behind a one-way mirror but you certainly see them in action as they respond to the creative material you and your staff have prepared.

Of course, what you find out is invaluable. But almost equally important is the use of the tapes as a selling tool. We are in an opinion business. There are no absolutes.

You have one opinion. The client has another. (And sometimes the client's wife has yet another.) When you can back up what you say with videotape segments of real consumers and real prospects, saying what they really believe in their own words, the effect can be devastating. You don't have to rig it with adroit editing. Just let the consumers tell the truth as they see it. The whole truth. And nothing but the truth.

There is a temptation sometimes to fudge it a little. To slant things just a bit. The client would probably never know.

Don't.

Don't even consider it. Your integrity is more important to your continued success than any other quality you possess. More than talent. More than thoroughness. More than anything.

Forgive me for preaching but your goal is to get the client to trust you and your agency. Once you have earned it, that trust is both precious and fragile. One breach of that trust and it's all over. No perceived short-term gain is worth that.

Want to make a marketing research person furious? Suggest we do "some quick and dirty research". I've seen some account types say that. I've seen the glare of hatred in return. You do it right. Or you don't do it.

And you tell the truth. No matter what. Okay? Okay.

There's one more reason I am so fond of focus groups. Not only did they prove invaluable in the creation of new advertising campaigns, but they also gave us a wonderful supply of quotes to spice up our research reports to the client. I remember three that still make me smile after all these years.

One night in Kansas City, our moderator Lu DiSalvo was trying to probe the "Cadillac mystique" and he asked this one middle-aged businessman the following question:

"What would you like your neighbors to think when you pull into your driveway with your brand new Cadillac?"

"That it's paid for," was his response.

We were in Los Angeles ending up one of our most important series of focus groups ever. This was the last of 28 sessions covering six different cities across the U.S. We wanted to make sure we were on the right track in introducing the new, smaller resized Cadillac's designed to yield better gas mileage after the traumatic energy crunch. Lu ended the session by asking the participants their final feelings about what they had heard and seen.

"I'll tell you this," said a surprisingly small Hollywood producer, "first thing tomorrow I'm going to call my Cadillac dealer and have him get me two more Fleetwood Broughams."

Two years later we were in Houston with a group of rather disgruntled Cadillac owners. They obviously were disenchanted with the new, resized Cadillac's. Finally one piped up to add a note of cheer. "I'll give them this," said this tall, tanned Texan. "They're peppy little cars."

CHAPTER SIX

The Pitch

The sales talk. The presentation. The pitch.

Call it what you will. It's the heart and soul of the advertising business. All business, for that matter.

An agency competitor of ours, N.W. Ayer, had a theme I've always admired. "Nothing happens until you make human contact." You could alter that to nothing happens until somebody makes a sales pitch. Because, in one way or another, that's what happens most of the time when we make human contact—doesn't it?

You know how many parts—key elements—there are to the pitch. Of course, three.

(1) Organization. (2) Practice. (3) Delivery.

Let's talk about organizing your pitch. Someone once said making an effective presentation consists of these three parts:

Tell them what you're going to tell them.

Tell them.

Tell them what you told them.

Very true. But there's more to it than that. There is a very simple form I have burned into my memory. With it, I can organize any talk on any subject—and do it on a single sheet of paper. And if I can do it, there's no reason you can't do it too.

Take a long, hard look at Figure 1. Start to burn it into your memory. Don't worry. Before long, it will be there forever. Let's fill in the boxes. In the top one, put the word "Opening". In the box right beneath that, the word "Subject". From left to right just above the next three rectangular boxes..."Agenda 1"..."Agenda 2"..."Agenda 3". Within the rectangles, left to right, put "Part 1"..."Part 2"..."Part 3". In the bottom tier of three boxes, write "Summary 1"..."Summary 2"..."Summary 3". And in the bottom box, write "Conclusion".

I suggest you run off a number of copies because you're going to be using it constantly. And, in the process, you're going to be automatically committing it to memory forever.

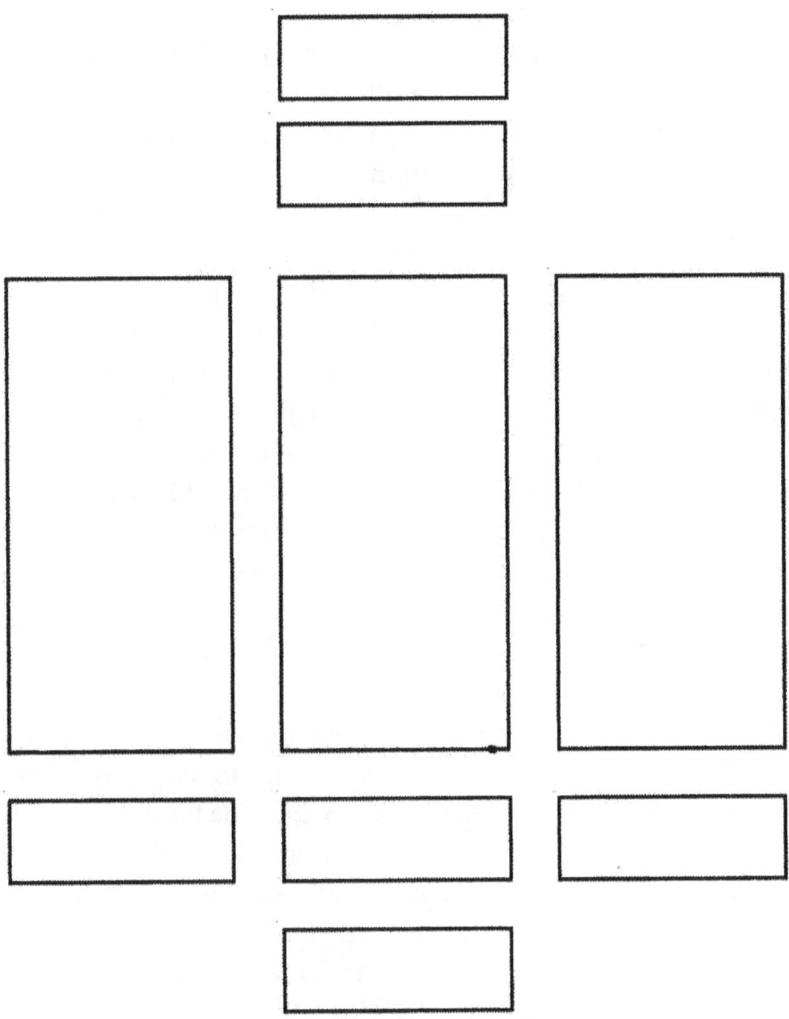

Figure 1

Now, let's put the form into action for that big pitch you have to make next Thursday morning. (Always try to make your presentations in the morning. You're fresher—and so is the client.)

Where do we start? With the second box down. Decide on your subject, topic or objective. What specifically are you going to cover—exactly. Leave no room for doubt with the client. It doesn't hurt to give it a title if that seems appropriate. The important thing is to decide exactly what your subject is and cover only that. Remember how annoyed you were the other day when Old Man Thomas rambled on and on…never getting to the point? Be thorough…be brief…be single-minded. Everyone will appreciate it—and you. Most especially the client.

Next thing to decide on…your agenda. To cover your subject or accomplish your objective, you're going to talk about three things, areas, parts, points, reasons, creative approaches, what-have-you. **THERE IS NO SUBJECT, HOWEVER INVOLVED OR COMPLEX, THAT CANNOT BE DIVIDED INTO THREE PARTS.** The more you work with this idea, the more you will become convinced it is true.

Okay, you've written down your subject and the three parts of your agenda. Now we're going to cover the meat of your presentation. Write down the one or two word heading for each part.

Under Part 1, list all the sub-points that substantiate your main point. Just a word or two to cue your memory. If you can keep it to three sub-points, that's good. But it's not essential. Do the same for Part 2 and Part 3.

After that, you want to tell them what you've told them. Write in a brief summary of each part in the bottom tier of boxes. Never cover new material here—only what you've presented.

Then, in the conclusion box jot down what you want your audience to do. What action do you want the client to take as a result of your presentation? *ASK FOR THE ORDER.* Nice people do, you know. The client expects it. Do it with conviction and enthusiasm.

Last to cover is the very first box on your form…the Opening. It can be any of a dozen different things but it should be relevant to your subject and never forced. It can be a humorous anecdote, a sports story, a strong quote or a historical analogy.

You can get the audience into the action by using a shocking statement, quote an authority or use a question that needs to be answered. Again, key your opening to your specific audience.

I have a little trick here that works for me. As you know, I'm opposed to memorization, but I find it helpful to memorize the first couple sentences of my opening. By getting me off on the right foot, it gives me a great feeling of confidence. Try it and see if it works for you.

To give you an idea how this whole outlining process works, let's figure one out together. By way of example, let's assume you've been asked to give a 20-minute talk on advertising to a class of first-year business college students at 10:35 a.m. next Tuesday. You've got plenty of other things to do before then so you can't spend much time in preparation. Yet, you welcome the chance to sharpen your presentation skills.

Enter your ever-faithful presentation outline. First, let's decide on your subject. What did you say? Sure, that a good title…"What every business person should know about advertising".

Next, let's figure out our agenda and write it down. That sounds good. Agenda 1…"What advertising is and what it includes". Agenda 2…"Who does it". Agenda 3…"How it works".

Now let's outline what we're going to cover under each.

Maybe something like this:

Part 1…**What it is and what it covers**
>   *What it is*
> . Average consumer subjected to 2,000 or more a day
> . Charmed by it…alarmed by it
> . Told by it…sold by it
> . Mass selling
> . Mass communication that somebody buys to sell a product, service or idea
> . It's big business (explain)

What it includes
. Newspapers
. Magazines
. Business/trade, paid/controlled
. TV
. Radio
. Outdoor
. Direct mail
. Specialty—airport, taxi
. Sales promotion/collateral
. The Internet

Part 2…Who does it
. In a way…everybody
. Leading advertisers
. Only 300,000 ad agency pros
. Broken up into
      —Creative
      —Account People
      —Media
      —Marketing
      —Production
      —Other

Part 3…How it works
. A case in point…introduction of the Seville (pick your own)
. Research results—pre and post
. Other examples

Next, of course, you summarize.
    . Advertising is mass selling and big business…includes all media
    . You know who does it from the creative team to final production

. And we've given you examples how it works

Then the conclusion.

. In conclusion, you now have some idea what every business person should know about that most persistent force in your life—advertising

Lastly, you tackle the opening. How about a riddle?

Maybe, something like this:

. Good morning. I have a riddle for you. What is the single, most persistent force in your life today? You see it and hear it every-where. Morning. Noon. Night.

It's brilliant. Terrible. Fascinating. Dull. Rewarding. Revolting.

Of course, it's _____.

There, you have it. Your trusty outline. Your golden guide that will give you courage and confidence. Your ready roadmap that will keep you on the subject and on time.

Now, back to that client presentation you have coming up. Let's say you have diagrammed your pitch on a single sheet of paper, now what? I suggest you make it easy on yourself and use a visual aids prop.

My overwhelming choice is a flip chart. It's highly effective…cheap…easy to use and easy to carry. Not only that, it allows you to maintain good eye contact throughout your presentation—unlike slides, for example.

I've seen and used every kind of flip chart from the four-color, highly elaborate variety to the rustic, black-and-white, economy model. In the end, it really doesn't matter. They all work.

To make your flip chart most effective, think like your client. Most of all, you want to be able to read it. So keep each page short and sweet with the lettering easy to see and read from the farthest reaches of the room. A good rule of thumb is: MAKE EACH LETTER AT LEAST 3 INCHES HIGH.

With that in mind, transfer the material from your outline to the flip chart—one chunk at a time. Any page too long? Break it up into two or three pages. Paper is cheap. Be sure to use a big thick magic marker—

black for your major lettering. Then, if you want to underline for emphasis, use red, blue or the color of your choice.

If you have access to an art director (or you're one yourself), you might want to dress it up a bit with a visual or graphic treatment throughout. But it really isn't necessary. You're the star of the show, not the flip chart. The chart is simply a tool to keep the client and you organized...on the subject...and on target.

Step Two: Practice...Rehearse. Using your flip chart and all other materials you'll be using, go through your presentation. Alone at first. In front of a mirror can be helpful. Videotape yourself if you can and take a close, honest look. Then, when you feel confident enough, make your presentation to a sympathetic friend or loved one. Keep at it...and before long the light will go on inside that head of yours. A little dim at first but stronger and stronger.

You know what you're talking about. You know how to make this presentation. You're going to be good. Good, hell. You're going to knock their socks off.

Once you start making presentations, stay at it. Do it every chance you get. Someone once said making pitches is like sex. The more you do it, the better you get. And the better you get, the more fun it is. I agree.

Step Three...Delivery. We can't cover everything but I have a few helpful hints for you.

First and foremost, realize you are not making a speech. Rather, you are delivering a communication. Experts in the communication skills business say a communication is a message given and received. It takes two to tango.

As such, you are ever aware of that client out there. Are you getting your point across? Is the client with you? Against you? Or not at home? Look at their eyes, their facial expressions, their body language.

The amazing thing is you can tell. Easily. The message is being received. Or it is not.

To be able to do this—to keep the two-way lines of communication open—you need to maintain good eye contact. So how do you do this? It's not a natural thing for most of us because we're taught as little ones it's not polite to stare. You're not staring, of course, but the feeling hangs on.

You do it by visiting—visiting each and every member of your audience for a period of five to ten seconds. Talk directly to one person. Look him/her right in the eyes, as if you were talking to this person alone. Turn to another person and do the same. Then to your far right, perhaps. The middle. The far left. Don't make too much of a pattern of it, but cover the entire room. As many times as you can.

All this sounds very forced. It is not after you get the feel of it. Try to make it very natural—not too regimented.

The surprising thing is each person then feels you are indeed talking directly to him or her—even when you're visiting someone else. Because he or she knows you're going to be returning…again and again. All great presenters have great eye contact.

The best presenters have another attribute you can develop. That's intensity. They know their subject. They're enthusiastic. And it shows. It's a far better thing to be too intense than too little. You believe in what you're presenting, don't you? Then show it.

One last thing, the effective presenter "owns his or her space". It is essential you feel totally at home in the area where you're presenting. You have to feel free to move to the right or left…to the front or rear of the room. You know where the light switches are and how to turn off that noisy air conditioner fan if you have to.

Obviously, it's important you spend some time in the presentation area prior to your big meeting. Do it by all means. Figure out exactly where the client will sit. Where you'll be presenting. Where your flip chart will be— before, during and after your presentation.

Most of all, you want to feel as comfortable and as confident as humanly possible.

You're ready. You've done your homework. Give 'em hell.

CHAPTER SEVEN

The Client

If you've ever worked on trying to get new business for an ad agency, you know what a rare and wonderful thing a good client is.

But, as a good wife, that good client can be taken for granted it you're not extremely careful. To paraphrase a World War II slogan—"The price of client satisfaction is eternal vigilance".

I've seen it happen time and time again...at big-time agencies and smaller shops. This business gets frustrating and tedious at times. Things go wrong and it's not your fault. You need a dog to kick. The client qualifies because he or she or it seems to be the source of much of your grief.

Meanwhile, the client has his share of problems and irritations. Life is seldom fair—even for clients. Things go wrong and it's not his/her fault either. He or she also needs a dog to kick. And the agency is so visible, so handy and in some ways so vulnerable.

Soon each side begins to kick a bit. Easily at first. Then with increasingly more bitterness.

What was once a happy client/agency marriage goes sour. And then you read all about it in AD AGE as the divorce becomes final.

Sadly, a good percentage of the time, it need not have happened.

As soon as the rumbling starts, however minor, immediate action should be taken. As agency people, our attitude should be: "Wait just one damn minute, Junior. This is our good client you are bad-mouthing. These are the people who pay our bills, including your salary. If you have a complaint, let's talk about it. If necessary, we'll get together with our good client and work things out".

It's just downright stupid to bite the hand that feeds you—isn't it?

Don't misunderstand me. I'm not talking about blind obedience or capitulation. That is equally stupid. The client hired us…and keeps paying us…because we provide a service he cannot provide for himself. When the day comes we become order-takers, divorce is again close at hand.

This may sound strange. But I've always believed in running a little scared. Are we really doing great work for this client? Is he/she pleased with us? Do we have any weaknesses in our relationship that we should be correcting? Are we covering ourselves at every level…most importantly at the top? Are we giving this client greater value than he can get from our competitors?

Again, I'm not talking about kissing butt. I'm talking about being an invaluable business partner to our client. I'm talking about mutual respect. I'm talking about being an equal in this marriage. And that, my friend, you earn.

Winning awards isn't the answer. How many times have you read about the agency that won top awards for the client one month and lost the business the next?

Winning new business on behalf of the client instead of awards for the agency is the answer. And being a friend. Not a country club phony but a real friend. Somebody you like and are genuinely concerned about.

A few years ago, I wrote something that expressed the feelings of some of us at DMB&B. You might find it helpful. I keep a copy clearly visible on my office wall in case I ever forget.

A CLIENT

A client is the most important person in our business.
A client is the lifeblood of this agency.

*A client always deserves our best effort, no matter what
the size of the account
or the billing on the individual job.
A client merits our courtesy and respect at all times.
A client is both our business partner and our boss, and as such, is entitled
to our total loyalty. But for the client's sake, we should never allow that loyalty
to cloud our judgment
or our creative integrity.
A client is as responsible for superior advertising as we are. Great advertising is as much a result of intelligent, imaginative and at times courageous
clients as it is a result
of brilliant work by the agency.
A client is a friend.*

CHAPTER EIGHT

The Ad Pro

A few years ago the managing director of our DMB&B/Bloomfield Hills office, Ron Monchak, asked me to do some thinking about a very basic question:

"What does it take to succeed in this advertising business?"

If we knew this, he said, it would help us in our hiring practices as well as enable us to do a better job in plotting career paths for our people. He felt I should have a handle on the subject because of my years of training our best young people as Chancellor of our "Brown Bag U." program. I had founded BBU six years earlier and it had turned out to be a great success.

I pondered the question. At first it seemed in the league of "What is life?" and "What does it take to be happy?". And the strains of those great old lyrics echoed in my brain—"How deep is the ocean…how high is the sky?".

But the more I thought about it…and the more I thought about the young men and women who had done well in BBU (as well as those who didn't)…a pattern began to take shape.

Within a few days, I had finalized my list and presented it to Ron. He agreed with the list and I think it might make sense to you.

What does it take to succeed in advertising? I'm convinced it takes a blend of these ten attributes—roughly in this order.

REQUIREMENTS OF THE GREAT AD PRO

1. **Enthusiasm.** Far and away, most important. Does that surprise you? It shouldn't. Nothing succeeds like enthusiasm. It is truly contagious, consuming all and conquering all. By enthusiasm, I mean a genuine love of what you are doing...a positive, winning attitude that emphasizes strengths and minimized weaknesses...a love of life.

At my retirement festivities Ron Monchak said I was blessed with passion. A passion for Brown Bag U...a passion for advertising...a passion for poetry...a passion for running...a passion for living. God, I loved his comment because it captured my philosophy in a single word. I responded by saying my Mother agreed with him. She often had said I overdid everything.

Passion...enthusiasm. With it, you can do almost anything. Without it, you are lost, in my view. I have run nine marathons since I turned age 52. Let me tell you, I'm not a natural athlete. I trained hard. But the most important part was mental.

First, you have to run the marathon—all 26 miles and 385 yards—in your mind. You have to be totally convinced you will do it. Notice I didn't say *can* do it. You *will* do it. Only that way can you—*will* you—overcome the pain, exhaustion and depression that creeps in after mile 15.

People like to be around enthusiastic people. They like to work with them. They are more willing to buy ideas from them. Enthusiasm...Number 1.

2. **Talent.** No doubt I am influenced greatly here by my creative director background. It is a cold, oftimes cruel fact that to succeed in the creative side of this business you must have talent. One of my most difficult tasks through the years was telling hard-working, dedicated young people they probably didn't have the talent to make it in ad agency creative work. To a degree, a certain level of pure talent is required for almost any job you can name in this business. It is not easy to honestly evaluate the raw talent you possess, but it is absolutely necessary to avoid the heartache that is sure to follow if you deceive yourself.

3. **A sense of humor.** There are times when I think it is the greatest gift any of us possess. Looking back, there were times I would have rated it

number one. A keen sense of humor—including the ability to laugh at yourself—can get you through almost anything.

One of the reasons I'm so high on a strong sense of humor is it foretells a solid sense of values. Most of all, it's our number one defense against taking ourselves too seriously.

I love to win in this business. I hate to lose. But in seeking new business, for example, you're committed to failure 95 percent of the time—no matter how good you are. So you damn well better use that sense of humor and use it often. To state the totally obvious—it makes you and everybody around you feel better.

For another thing, a keen sense of humor is a terrific selling tool. It can make the client look forward to hearing what you have to say…and sell.

As for taking myself too seriously, I always had a working philosophy that goes something like this. On one hand, I realize this is a big, serious business involving millions of dollars. On the other hand, I know in my heart of hearts it's a game. Even though it is not brain surgery, I will give it my damndest to win. But deep down—win or lose—I know it is a game.

Without half trying, I can name a hundred things more important than advertising. And so can you. Keep that sense of humor and that sense of values intact. No matter what.

4. **People-smarts.** You could call it the ability to get along with people…to work effectively with other people…to get people to buy what you are selling. Experience has convinced me that people-skills are far more important than pure intelligence. Although it probably can be argued people-smarts is a part of intelligence.

Every survey I have seen on the subject states most people don't lose their jobs in advertising (or any other business) because of a lack of talent or determination or I.Q. They fail because they couldn't get along with people. Makes sense—doesn't it?

5. **Stamina.** You've heard me say it before and I'm going to say it again. This is tough business. You have to be strong, tenacious and resilient to

make it long-term. And I'm not talking only about strong mentally. You must be strong physically to put in the time and effort it takes.

About ten years ago I hired a wonderfully-gifted young art director but I did it with misgivings. Claudia seemed to be the perfect choice for our needs but she was so small...so delicate...so almost frail. We took a chance and in the beginning she did seem to tire easily. And then—slowly at first—a remarkable thing happened. Our Claudia toughened up. Today she is managing both a family and a career. And doing it beautifully. She still looks delicate but she is one tough ad person.

6. **Curiosity**. The great ad pro is always curious...always wondering how things work...what would happen if we did this instead of that...always thinking about what motivates people to do what they do, say what they say, buy what they buy. It is, I guess, the natural curiosity of the child's mind that fortunately has never been dulled by the journey into adulthood.

I am no longer young. This gives a little perspective. I can look back and see all those dumb questions weren't dumb at all. But sometimes the answers were. What was once good for us is now bad for us...and the reverse.

I am more curious now than I ever was. (Many of my friends would agree with that statement.) Knowledge is doubling every ten years. Knowledge—not wisdom. More answers lead to ever more questions. I am convinced we are barely at the beginning in this quest instead of nearing the end.

As much as we know, we know very little. A friend of mine likes to say: "We don't know a damn thing about nothing." He could have a point.

Six months prior to the Wright brothers doing their thing, the world's leading authority on flight said man would never be able to fly. Not much has changed.

7. **Determination**. I look up again at that cheap little plague on my wall. Its simple message has touched my soul many a time. So much so that I've given away hundreds of copies after my talks at colleges and elsewhere. You might want to pin a copy on your wall—for those difficult days when you wonder why you ever got into this business.

PRESS ON
NOTHING
IN THE WORLD CAN
TAKE THE PLACE OF PERSISTENCE.
TALENT WILL NOT; NOTHING IS MORE
COMMON THAN UNSUCCESSFUL MEN
WITH TALENT. GENIUS WILL NOT;
UNREWARDED GENIUS IS ALMOST
A PROVERB
EDUCATION ALONE WILL NOT;
THE WORLD IS FULL OF EDUCATED
DERELICTS. PERSISTENCE AND
DETERMINATION ALONE ARE
OMNIPOTENT.

"Persistence and determination alone are omnipotent". How true. You have to want it so bad you're willing to pay the price to get it. And sometimes that price can be pretty high. I remember three times I hired a creative person almost solely because that person didn't give up. In the end, I figured if they were so hell-bent on getting the job they must be convinced they could handle it. And in the process I became convinced. All three have done well.

8. **Education**. Getting a good, well-rounded education is part of that price you have to pay to succeed in this business. Taking advertising and journalism courses can be extremely helpful but I certainly wouldn't stop there. Reach out. Expand your horizons. Learn much about many things. As I look back, I can't recall ever taking any college course on any subject that didn't turn out to be useful somewhere along the way.

A case in point, I registered late one semester at Oberlin College and ended up with little choice in courses. Begrudgingly, I signed up for something called Bibliography X-3. It turned out to be one of the most valuable courses I ever took. Bibliography X-3 covered the history of type.

Later in my career, copywriters, art directors and sometimes clients were impressed by what I knew about Caslon, Bodoni and such.

9. **Common sense**. I've always preferred it to pure intelligence. Maybe you've heard the story but it bares repeating. Three strangers were traveling across the country on an airplane—a priest, a hippie and the smartest man in the world. Suddenly the plane lost both engines and started to go down. But when the three looked around there were only two parachutes. The smartest man in the world said, "I really feel bad about this, but I must save my intellect for the good of mankind". And in an instant, he jumped. Turning to the hippie, the priest said, "I am a man of God, my son, so I want you to jump".

"Don't worry about it, Father," said the hippie. "The smartest man in the world grabbed my knapsack!"

I've seen it happen time and again. We've even coined a name for it. "Analysis paralysis". Academic intelligence alone can be a trap in this business. Nine times out of ten, we are trying to influence ordinary people…not PHDs. Ron Monchak puts is well: "Most of us who make it in this business are ordinary people doing extraordinary things."

10. **Courage**. Call it nerve, grit or guts. If you stay in advertising, there will come a time when you are tested. There will come a time when you must draw upon that courage that dwells deep within you. Permit me please to be a little corny. Using courage doesn't mean you're necessarily going to win. Sometimes, my friend, it means almost certain defeat. By courage, I'm talking about doing the right thing…by taking a course of action that makes you proud of you. There is no reward greater than that.

Be strong. Be firm. Be friendly. Be brave.

You're an ad pro.

CHAPTER NINE

The Miracle

I have seen many things during my 35 plus years in the advertising business. On a number of occasions, I have seen us snatch defeat from the jaws of victory. And the opposite.

I have seen greatness…and pettiness…and everything in between.

But I have seen only one genuine miracle. And that took place in a most unlikely setting—Youngstown, Ohio. Looking back, I have to believe what made the miracle so significant was the magnitude of the disaster that proceeded it.

At first, everything seemed to be going beautifully. We were only one step away from landing a meaningful piece of new business—the Youngstown Steel account. For several months now we had worked closely with the advertising manager and his six-person staff. Let's call him Mike.

The final step was our presentation to top management and Mike was a tremendous help to us in preparing for the big day. We worked our buns off. We wanted this one…bad. At last we were ready. We phoned Mike and he set it up for 10 a.m. Thursday. According to plan, we had our last rehearsal at the agency in Bloomfield Hills, Michigan on the day before, and set off by car and station wagon to arrive in Youngstown for dinner and a good night's sleep. The next morning at 8:30 a.m. we joined Mike and his staff for a final run-through prior to the big show.

Nobody knows how it happened. Catastrophe. Somehow the tops of the slide trays had twisted off and the boxes had been overturned. It was a holy mess.

Our AV guy, Ted Roy-Bob Cram, did the best he could for the final rehearsal with Mike.

It was terrible. More than half the slides were in the wrong order. Now there was less than half an hour till the biggies walked in.

Mike was beside himself. It was too late to call the whole thing off. But it was obvious a screw-up like this wasn't going to do his career any good.

There was shouting. Bitter words were exchanged. Then silence. The only sound you could here was that splashing sound of client people leaping out of the canoe.

We left Ted alone to salvage what he could. I was sick and angry. It wasn't fair. Screw this business.

9:56 a.m. The big five arrive. Mike is trying his best to smile. I am wishing I were somewhere else. Anywhere else.

The lights dim.

The show is on.

Mike begins his part. The first slide appears on the screen on cue. It dissolves to the second. The third. The fourth.

It seems to me, Mike is gaining a small measure of confidence. Maybe, dear God, at least his section will be okay. I notice I am digging the fingernails of my right hand into my leg. Enough of that.

Soon Mike is mercifully finishing his part. Almost with a small flourish, it seems to me.

But his part is nothing in complexity and length compared to Chuck's and mine.

You know how it must be when you know you cannot win…that no matter what you do, you're going to die? Right, you don't give a rat's ass. You play with reckless abandon.

Chuck did.

And then I did. Slide after slide. Perfect.

Chuck was great.

I was great.

We had pitched a perfect game!

Now the lights were on. And these five hardened men of the world were applauding. I mean—standing on their feet and slapping their hands together.

After the kind words and warm handshakes, I walked back to the little screening room at the rear of the auditorium. I slowly opened the door and there was Ted. He was sitting on a stool. Staring. Just staring straight ahead as if he was in shock. He couldn't believe what had just happened anymore than I could. Perfect. The bloody thing was perfect.

Through the years since that morning in Youngstown, Ohio, Ted and I have shared many a drink together at many an agency function. Almost every time we do, we talk about it. And we agree. There's only one explanation for what happened.

It was a miracle.

CHAPTER TEN

The Politics

The first thing you have to realize is there's always politics.

At some agencies and some offices, it's worse than others. But it's always there.

Therefore, if you're in the advertising business now or planning to make it your career, you should know something about office politics and how to play the game.

Let me tell you right off I've always prided myself on being a loner. It's not that I don't like people individually or in small groups. I dislike being part of a large group and I treasure my privacy. Feeling this way, I thought at first I could ignore the whole political scene. Damn it, I'd do my work well and let that speak for me. It wasn't long before experience convinced me that course of action was a mistake.

You have to play the game to succeed. And to play well, you have to know the rules.

Rule 1: Know the agency pecking order…stated and real. Start with the obvious. I've never worked for an agency that didn't have a T.O. Study the table of organization for your agency. It's almost always out of date but commit it to memory anyway. You will find it useful. While memorizing it, make sure you learn the correct spelling of all key players. You will find that exceedingly helpful, too.

Another hint. Save all agency memos. Although most are a frightful bore, they can reveal important clues as to what's going on. Even such mundane items as who receives copies of what memos on what subjects for which accounts.

Okay, that's the stated pecking order. For the real world, again start with the obvious. Nothing can tell you more faster with greater accuracy than agency housing. It is more structured than the Chinese army. Where does somebody stand? Look at where he or she sits. Look at his or her office.

Here's how it goes in order of rank.

. No office.	Clerical, beginner or somebody on the way out.
. Shared office.	Senior clerical or promising beginner.
. Small private inside office sans window and carpet.	Junior account person or creative novice.
. Large private office with carpet but sans window.	Younger account exec, creative on the way up or senior on the way down.
. Small outside office with window.	Established art director, copywriter or account person.
. Larger outside office with window, carpet and original oil painting.	Senior art director, established copywriter or senior account person.
. Much larger outside office with several windows, carpet, paintings and own conference table.	Group head or high company officer.
. All of above plus secretary in adjacent office.	Managing director of the office or equivalent.

We human animals have a fetish for demonstrating our territorial rights and rites. Nowhere is it more obvious than in ad biz. Especially at the agency level. At DMB&B/Bloomfield Hills, it was carried to the ultimate. The whole top third floor was occupied by only management people and their secretaries. Up there the offices were larger, the carpet thicker, the air cooler in the summer and warmer in the winter. People spoke in hushed tones. You had the feeling that, if there were a heaven where good and faithful ad folks went, it would be like this.

I always felt the structure was unfortunate. It was so easy to develop what came to be known at "the third floor syndrome". The isolation seemed to breed an escape from reality and a false sense of infallibility.

Then again, it could be sour grapes. The highest I ever rose was to a large corner office with carpet, windows and paintings on the second floor. I never made it to the hallowed third floor.

Rule 2: Have a game plan. It works in football and it works in this business. Make *you* your client and decide what you want to be, where you want to go, how much money you want to make and how you propose to do all this.

Put it in writing. Exactly what are your goals and how can you make them reality…short term and long term? They'll change, of course, from time to time but it's amazing what happens when you **put it in writing**. It clarifies fuzzy thinking. This simple action forces you to make decisions…which in turn forces you to take action.

Somehow we get the idea it's okay to plan careers for others but not ourselves. That's stupid…isn't it?

Rule 3: Treat everybody with dignity and respect. An old boss of mine, Pete Moore, used to say: "The ribbon clerks of today are the movers and shakers of tomorrow."

He's right, of course. But there's more to it than that. It's not just it's to your advantage to do so, they deserve it. And it makes you feel good.

A number of years ago, I was an arrogant bastard. Then something happened that woke me up. My wife and I adopted a two-year-old boy who "had problems". He was said to be a slow learner and he had been misused by his real mother, as well as by some of his foster parents prior to his coming to us.

Today George has carved out a life for himself and we are very proud of him. But he went through hell to get there. And we went through hell. Along the way, he spent some time in a state hospital or two. Where he was abused again. It tore our hearts out. But in going through it all, I learned something.

I learned a little compassion. I learned we are all God's children. The strongest and most secure of us are feeble and weak. Our journey on this earth is frightfully short.

I learned we all need each other.

I am not quite as arrogant as I used to be. Yes, I try to treat everybody with dignity and respect. And so should you.

Rule 4: Know the rules and use them to your advantage. There is a right way and a wrong way to do almost anything in this business. Doing it the right way saves your time and works better. How's that for a totally obvious comment?

Here's what I mean. You're the copy chief and you have a new assignment for one of your writers. Should you go to his office or call and have him come to your place? Dumb question…doesn't matter? Wrong.

You should call and have him come to your office. It's so much smoother all around and saves time and potential problems. Also, it clarifies the structure. You are the copy chief and he is the writer.

All this sounds silly as hell but it is not. Shortly after I became copy chief, I thought it would be democratic and a goodwill gesture if I went to my writers' offices to give assignments and critique their material. What a mess. It plain didn't work.

I also tried that democratic approach after I became an officer in the Marine Corps. It didn't work there either.

Know the rules and play by them.

Rule 5. Get involved. As a born-again loner, giving this advice goes against the grain. But it makes sense.

A few years ago, I found myself on no less than seven different agency committees. I don't know how it happened but this loner wasn't one anymore. And I was having more fun and influencing more people than I ever had before. All of which was good for the career.

In short, let them see you in action…often. Take every opportunity to demonstrate your skills. If there's a training program, for God's sake apply. If you're too advanced for that, volunteer to be a teacher.

Getting involved makes the old ad game a lot more fun…and a lot more profitable.

Rule 6: Never suffer in silence. If you think you've been wounded, say something about it to somebody who can do something about the situation.

But…wait a day. Please don't do it in anger. That's good advice I personally find hard to take. There's nothing more soul-satisfying than to strike back in anger. "Vengeance is mine," saith the Lord. It feels so good. But it can do us in.

After that day of cooling down passes and you're still convinced you have been treated shabbily, prepare your case like the ad pro you are. Not "I've been hurt and it's not fair". Rather make it "These actions have adversely affected my performance and my contributions to this agency."

The more professional and non-personal you can be, the more effective you will be. To do this, I urge you to plan your presentation with great care. Rehearse it well. Make your appointment to present your case. And present it in a firm, friendly and professional manner. You'll be glad you did.

Rule 7: Be true to you. As a creative director, I often said I worked first for the consumer, second for the client and thirdly for the agency.

Yet, in a sense, this is not true. Most of all, I worked for me. Most important of all, I had to please me…to meet my creative standards. In the end, you work for yourself.

There is a saying: "People will treat you the way you insist they treat you." There is some truth to it. When you are true to yourself and what you believe, it comes through. Other people get the message.

You're no phony. No shallow, arm-twisting back-stabber. No brown-nosing ass-kisser.

You're an ad pro…and proud of it.

CHAPTER ELEVEN

The Word

One of my all-time favorite movies is "The Graduate". And my favorite scene is where this older guy whispers the magic word to Dustin Hoffman…the one word that's going to make his future bright and rosy.

"Plastics," he says with reverence. "Plastics."

I love it. And throughout my career in advertising, that scene replays itself in my mind's eye…time and time again.

The secret is…

(Your favorite magical word goes here).

It can be high drama…as it was in "The Graduate". And in real life.

A few years ago, we had an earthquake on the Cadillac account. It registered an eight on the Richter Scale. General Motors replaced the top gun at Cadillac. Gone was the General Manager who was a known quantity, a friend of the agency, a defender of good advertising, a force we could count on to sell the good stuff.

His replacement was an unknown quantity and that was frightening enough. Add to that the fact the country was going through its first big oil crisis and sales of luxury cars were dwindling.

We soon learned Bob Lund was going to be a force to be reckoned with. To say he was high-powered and energetic would be the understatement of the century.

He was intense. Our advertising meetings were intense. Mr. Lund (only later were some of us allowed to call him Bob) was totally committed to turning things around at Cadillac…oil crisis or no. And you know damn well all of us in the agency shared his commitment. Nobody more than the creative director on the Cadillac account…one George A. Scott.

We had morning meetings. Afternoon meetings. Saturday meetings. At Cadillac. At the agency. And one time at a hotel ballroom.

These were tough days. Bob, excuse me, Mr. Lund, suggested I have our creative team make up little tent cards to place before everybody who sat in on the Cadillac Advertising Committee meetings…about 12 in all. I still have mine.

In brilliant three colors, it states:

"WE'RE IN A FULL COURT PRESS. LET'S KEEP IT UP!"

To say the pressure was on me as creative director would itself be an understatement. I would leave those meetings utterly exhausted. Everybody did.

Mr. Lund took his job very seriously. And we took Mr. Lund very seriously.

Example: One afternoon I was making a creative presentation before the Cadillac Advertising Committee. At a critical point during my pitch, Mr. Lund grabbed a pencil, scribbled a note and passed it to the general sales manager on his left. He read it, jotted a response and passed it quickly back to Mr. Lund who read it, crumpled it and dropped it to the floor.

Although accomplished discretely, the proceedings did not go unnoticed. I, for one, wondered what the hell was going on. But the real ad pro stays calm, cool, collected. At least on the outside.

After the meeting, which went better than we anticipated, and our Cadillac guests had gone, we breathed a collective sigh of relief. Then Pete Moore and I got the same idea at the same time. He reached the note first, opened it, and read it aloud.

"Who's the tall guy at the end of the table?" had asked Mr. Lund.

"George Harlund, our new Assistant National Merchandising Manager," was the reply. So much for intrigue.

Those were days more pleasant to recall than experience. And I can't remember them at all without thinking of a word. Bob Lund's favorite word. The single word he felt was the true measure of effective advertising.

I cringe even yet as I say it aloud.

The word is…

Bite.

Let me restate that.

The word is…

BITE!!!

"Does that ad you just presented have bite, George?" he would ask. How do you answer a question like that?

We would counter with agency jargon. "Testing indicates we're in the top ten percentile in stopping power, etc., etc." He was not always impressed.

In the final analysis, the judge of whether an ad had bite or not—and if it did, how much—was Bob Lund.

His point was, of course, well taken. To be effective, advertising does have to get attention. It does have to cut though the clutter…provoke interest…and evoke action. It can't just soothe the prospect or entertain him or her…it has to do something. Get him into the showroom to take a test-drive, ideally.

Makes sense, doesn't it. In all truth, my Bob Lund days weren't much fun but they did help me sharpen my advertising skills. Bite will do that.

The power of a single word. I still marvel in it. Somebody says the word "excitement" and I immediately think of Pontiac.

"Luxury"…Cadillac.

"Beef"…Wendy's.

"Glad"…Wrap.

And on it goes. Put two words together or three and the game is endless.

But sometimes an off-the-beaten-path word can bring back a whole series of images in living color. Such a word for me is…

"Gestalt."

Gestalt. According to Webster: "A structure or configuration of physical, biological, or psychological phenomena so integrated as to constitute a functional unit with properties not derivable from its parts in summation."

Wow. I'm not sure I grasp all that. Nor am I sure Mike did. Remember Mike? He was ad manager at Youngstown Steel when the miracle occurred.

"Advertising has to have *gestalt*, " he would say. He always paused before he said the word and infused it with a heavy German accent. I was impressed. The whole agency account team was.

Later I wondered. Could an ad have both bite and gestalt?

Another word from another era with a whole other message...

"concern".

More specifically:

"social concern".

Back in the 60s, a giant of a man who was far ahead of his time, called for a conference with his advertising agency. The man: A. P. Fontaine, CEO and Chairman of the Board of Bendix Corporation. The agency: MacManus, John and Adams of Bloomfield Hills (predecessor to DMB&B).

It developed Mr. Fontaine was deeply concerned about the problems facing the country at that time and believed a large company such as Bendix had a corporate responsibility to become involved. For advertising people, not noted for idealism, this might be hard to swallow. But I am totally convinced he had no other motive than the one he stated.

The ground rules were simple and direct: There were to be no commit-tees on this campaign. He would sit down with one agency person—the writer. All details—from discussion of ad topics to approval of four-color proofs—would be handled through meetings between Mr. Fontaine and the writer. That writer turned out to be me.

Perhaps you remember the ads. Covering such subjects as drug abuse, the generation gap and the age of majority, they ran for several years in TIME, NEWSWEEK and other national print media.

Long before the words social concern became a cliché in this business, this man had the guts to speak up and speak out about things that mattered—without seeking direct corporate gain.

Depending upon your point of view, it was either a foolish, wasteful exercise or a wise and courageous one. Not surprising, I lean to the latter.

Reading the hundreds and thousands of letters received in response made me believe that along the way the ads made a lot of friends for Bendix.

When A. P. retired, I was pleased to be asked to create a plague on behalf on Bendix Corporation to honor him. It read:

In recognition of A. P. Fontaine upon his retirement as Chairman of the Board and Chief Executive Officer of the Bendix Corporation March Twenty-ninth, Nineteen Hundred and Seventy-two.

The man made his mark.

For the better part of a decade it was he who set the goals that were to reshape and revitalize the corporation. And time and time again it was his leadership that made these goals reality.

He did much. Yet, those who know him best appreciate even more the way he did these things.

His decisive leadership...his integrity...his quiet, good humor...his love of life and hatred of sham.

It is no small wonder that for a whole generation of people, Bendix is A. P. Fontaine. A. P. Fontaine is Bendix.

I have another reason for including this tribute to a guy I obviously admire. In all humility, I believe it is a good example of what I preach. Good writing is clear...concise...simple.

There is so much bullshit in the world that the clear, simple stuff stands out. It is honest, sincere, to the point. Rare indeed in today's world.

Because of the word challenge, I guess, I have developed a special fondness for writing plaques and tributes of every kind. Even today I reread them with a sense of pride you may find quaint. Bendix, for example. Not only did I write the tribute for the client, I also wrote the one on behalf of the agency.

In appreciation to A. P. Fontaine:

Many of the ads we are proudest of owe their effectiveness to his ideas and his concern for the common good.

D'Arcy-MacManus Advertising

April 21, 1972

I just figured out yet another reason why I love tributes so much. Print ads and TV commercials come and go but plaques hang on somebody's wall forever.

CHAPTER TWELVE

The Job

Now you have to understand I was never afraid of hard work. No one was in our family. In fact, my two sisters, (Doris and Olive), later my younger brother Ron and I were well indoctrinated with the traditional middle class work ethic.

At the evening dinner table, Dad would often say to me (being the oldest): "Well, George, did you have a productive day today?' Not, "Did you have a good day?" and never "Did you have a fun day?". We used to make fun of that when we were growing up. But, by God, I have turned into my old man…at least in some ways. Every now and then I find myself saying the same bloody thing to my wife Jil: "I really had a productive day today—how about you?"

If I had any illusions that advertising would be anything but hard work after a guy by the name of Bob Byrd hired me away from THE MARION STAR (President Warren G. Harding's old newspaper in Marion, Ohio), I was soon set straight. Along with serving as copy contact on several accounts, my main job at a medium–size agency called Jay H. Maisch Advertising was to publish six house organs. Now I use the term "publish" very loosely. I did everything but print them myself.

They consisted of three externals and three internals and I never worked so hard in my life. I was responsible for everything, beginning with meeting with the client to map out the basics of the next issue for each. Then I would prepare a list of subjects with a description of each for client approval…gather material including interviewing employees, customers and others in the process…write the copy and headlines…create an interesting layout to make sure it would all fit…present it to the client prior to turning it over to the printer…proofread the silverprints (or other material supplied by the printer)…get the client to do the same, routing it through key personnel…make whatever changes necessary and rewrite material where required…check to make sure the printer made the changes correctly…and finally check the final product as it came off the press. Plus…

I even learned how to use a Speed Graphic camera so I could take my own photographs.

Which I did on a regular basis. Talk about work. It was a killer. But together with my newspaper background, it taught me how to write well and to make key decisions quickly under pressure. It also taught me the basics of layout design—enough to fortify me against being conned by a devious art director later in my career.

Then I did a dumb thing. Attracted by more money and a new brick home in Midland, Michigan, I went over to the other side of the desk and joined the advertising staff of The Dow Chemical Company. Millard Hooker, Dow Advertising Manager, immediately told me what my job was not. It was not to be creative. He said and I quote accurately:

"If you are caught doing creative work of any kind, you will be fired! That's the agency's job."

End of discussion. Interestingly, Dow's agency was MacManus, John & Adams, the very agency I was to join as a creative director after a seven-and-a-half year tour of duty at Barnes Chase Advertising in San Diego.

I hated it at Dow. Not the company but the job. Telling me I couldn't do any creative work was like telling a singer not to sing…a painter not to paint.

So Jil and I sold our lovely brick house in Midland, Michigan, auctioned off all our worldly goods except a few clothes and our car and headed west. Because Jil and I had mailed out resumes and hand-typed sales letters to over 100 agencies and companies in the area, I got two job offers on the second day after we arrived. One from a company and one from an agency. I took the agency offer.

Again, my job at Barnes Chase was tough in serving as copy/contact on ten (sometimes more) accounts but I loved it. I was back in creative again.

But for personal reasons, we finally sold off everything and headed back to Michigan. My first stop was—yes—MacManus, John & Adams (to later become D'Arcy, Masius, Benton & Bowles). After extensive interviewing I got the job. Now I was not only back in creative, I was in the Big Leagues. But could I handle this? I had the self-doubts of a rookie outfielder making the giant leap from the Class D Marion Red Sox to the mother club in Boston. Now I was working with the best in the world—competing against the best in the world. MJ&A accounts included Cadillac, Pontiac, Dow, GMAC, Kirsch, etc.

My last interview to seal the job for me was with the agency creative director Chuck Felt. He was a handsome, sophisticated guy who impressed the hell out of me. He was an advertising legend throughout the Midwest. In fact, he was the guy who created that TV advertising classic that featured Dom Delouise making a pitch for Koepplinger's Bread. Maybe you remember it.

At the end of the commercial, Dom says.

"Koepplinger's Bread. Let me spell it for you.

"B–R–E–A–D"

As I showed Chuck my portfolio, including two 250-page books I had created and written on NLS Digital Voltmeters (an early distant cousin to computers), I honestly don't think he thought all that much of my creative ability but I do think I impressed him with the fact that I was a hard worker.

"Ok," he said. "You're hired. You'll be the creative director on Bendix and I want to tell you this right now.

"Your job is to keep Chuck Howson off my ass!"

Chuck Howson was the account supervisor on Bendix and one tough hombre. As I was soon to discover many, if not most, MJ&A people actually feared him. In fact, the guy who was creative director on Bendix before me committed suicide. I'm not sure it was a direct result of working with Howson but I'm equally sure it didn't help.

Well, after two hitches in the Marine Corps I didn't frighten easily. I made up my mind that I was going to give the job my very best and take no crap from Howson. I think some humans are like dogs—they can smell fear.

It turned out that Howson and I got along fine. He did his job and I did mine. We respected each other. I and my team of writers and art directors made him look good. And I liked the way Howson fought for his client…Bendix. Despite everything else, he wanted nothing but the best for his client. And I felt the same way.

A month went by and I didn't even see Chuck Felt until one day I ran into him in the men's room.

"Oh yeah, Scott—isn't it? I wanted to tell you that you must be doing a good job. Chuck Howson hasn't been on my ass since you took over."

I was on cloud nine. That had to be one of the finest compliments I had ever received.

I was doing the job. I was making it in the Big Leagues.

CHAPTER THIRTEEN

The Tricks Of The Trade

I wish I had known somebody like me when I was somebody like you—young and anxious about making it big in the advertising business. It would have saved me huge amounts of time and grief.

Lucky you. You've got me—to reveal those little tricks of the trade that I had to learn the hard way. You just can't spend 35 plus years creating advertising without finding out what works…and what doesn't.

Trifles they are. But tremendous trifles they can be if they help make you a better ad person and make your work that much more effective.

No, they are not profound. Yes, they can be potent. And they're easy to remember and apply.

BE NARROW-MINDED. Nothing kills readership faster in print than wide columns of type. Nothing stops viewer interest faster in a TV or radio spot than wall to wall words. Don't try to reach too far—to appeal to too many different facets of your market. Key in on your bull's eye person and the rest will follow.

TRUST YOUR GUT. Your head (logic) tells you one thing but your gut (intuition) tells you something else. Go with your gut. The truth is *my gut has never been wrong.* Once, I ignored what my gut was trying to tell me. At the time I was trying to add another writer to my team and I wasn't having much success. In my haste, I talked myself into hiring a guy I knew wasn't right. Six months later I had to fire him. It was a messy business. Even his mother called me from Tennessee to tell me how cruel I was. I wasn't cruel…just dumb. I hadn't trusted my good old reliable gut.

LOVE THOSE WIDOWS. You know what widows are—those one or two words that carry over to the next line in a column of type. Ad school used to teach that you should try to eliminate them to give the copy a crisp, clean look. Wrong. Widows help break up a copy block, giving the eye a welcome break to make for better readership.

KILL YOUR DARLINGS. We all have them—those clever, folksy or familiar phrases or ideas that we just have to include. "It's too good to leave out," we reason. Does it track exactly with your message? Leave it in. If it doesn't, kill it.

SORRY, MRS. SHOE. She was my English teacher in the seventh grade and, let me tell you, nobody made fun of her name. She was tough. Woe to him or her who didn't follow the rules of English exactly. She was death on incomplete sentences, dangling participles and such. Sorry, Mrs. Shoe. But I am convinced the best way to communicate—to reach people and keep their attention is to write the way you speak. Correct English, of course. But conversational English. Make that conversational American.

CUT THROUGH WITH CUTLINES. People love to read the words that go under a picture—especially if you keep them short. They'll read cutlines when they won't read anything else. Take advantage of it. Work hard on your cutlines to make them carry the heart of your message.

STOPPING POWER IS NO. 1. You know it. I know it. Everybody knows it. Unless you stop that viewer or reader, the game is over before it begins. You have to stop them, get their attention, cut through the clutter. That's the creative challenge and there's an unlimited number of ways to do it. Some people scream "SEX". Or try to shock the prospect in some other way. Experience has convinced me the best way is not through gimmicks or trickery. The best way to reach anybody is through his or her own self-interest. And to do that with a fresh, innovative approach that's believable.

YOU'VE GOT TO BELIEVE. Once you stop them, you face that other monumental challenge. You must get consumer interest and involvement while building desire for the product or service—none of which can happen without believability. Do you know how difficult that is in today's world? Who believes advertising anyway? It's all lies—isn't it? Not all. A few ads and companies are respected, listened to and believed. It's your job to create ads that are among those precious few.

ADMIT IT. Sometimes confession can be good for the soul…and the ad. Owning up to what appears to be a negative can help to substantiate your positive points. The consumer reasons this way: "If the company is honest enough to tell me the negative, chances are the rest of what they say is true." Of course, it must be done adroitly but it can be effective. An example from a brochure I wrote recently: "Some people say we carry the quality idea to extremes…that we are fanatics about it. They could be right…"

GIVE 'EM A GOODIE. What you say last in your message is important because that's the lasting impression the consumer will take with her or him. It could make the difference whether the ad evokes action or not. Give 'em a goodie—a little reward for reading or listening to what you have to say. Try it. It works.

DON'T FENCE ME IN. You can be a proud, honest professional in this business without being an arrogant ass about it. Advertising is an art…not a science. There are many ways to solve a problem. Do your work and you will end up with one approach you believe is best. But don't fence the client in. Give the client your best three solutions. If the client picks any of the three, it's victory. Because you made sure all three were excellent pieces of work.

WHEN YOU'RE STUCK… You've hit a brick wall. You're dead in the water. Nothing works. I know the feeling. Because it happens to everybody sometime. Don't sweat it. Do realize it happens to the best of us. So relax. Do something else. Take a walk, run, go shopping. When you return, think about talking it over with somebody you respect. Talking helps. Then sit down and begin. Don't force it. Put something down on paper. Anything. Look at it. How can you improve it? Good. Now work on that. Something beats the hell out of nothing. Start with a 2 x 4, work with it, add to it and before long you end up with a house. If you don't like that house, build another. That's how the creative thing works sometimes. You work your tail off creating things and then throw away everything but the good stuff. It doesn't matter you took a little longer to get there. You got there.

CHAPTER FOURTEEN

The Trap

Put a wild animal in a cage for an extended period and a strange thing happens. When you try to give him his freedom, he often refuses to leave his prison.

We humans show similar tendencies.

Time and again in the advertising business we allow ourselves to end up in the trap. And we eventually become content to stay there.

To avoid the trap, let's talk about its many shapes and forms…beginning with the most common and the most cruel.

THE SEX TRAP. If I were a female in the advertising business, I probably would operate in varying stages of rage. The truth is women do not receive equal pay for equal work—nor do they have the same opportunities for advancement as men.

Yes, the situation has improved in the last 25 years but the sex trap is still very real. As chairman of our agency Morale Subcommittee, I suggested we conduct a survey of employee beliefs and attitudes in many areas. Guess what we discovered year after year. Not only did women not believe they didn't receive equal pay and opportunity for advancement—men also agreed women didn't get a fair shake. Year after year, survey results were the same. We all talked about it but nothing much seemed to change.

A case in point. DMB&B/Bloomfield Hills was basically run by the Management Committee that varies between ten and fourteen members. Until the day I retired, there never was a female member. Not one.

Yet, in all fairness, DMB&B was much more liberal in its policies toward women than many agencies. There has been much improvement. People do try. It is just very difficult to change attitudes ingrained since birth.

Women themselves are somewhat to blame, in my opinion. They just don't raise enough hell—long enough or loud enough in the right places and the right way. Maybe because it's not ladylike.

The agency business is a reflection of the entire advertising business—all business and American society for that matter. The sex trap is everywhere.

How can we combat it? I have thoughts on that subject.

First, don't let them label you. A label can be the kiss of death. And one of the worst labels for an female ad pro can be "Secretary". It closes the door to the sex trap faster than almost anything else.

I feel so sorry for women who have done exceedingly well in college, earned their degree and then in a tight job market, go to work as secretaries on "a temporary basis". A few break out. Many do not. And the longer they remain as secretaries—and the better the job they do—the stronger the trap.

One who did have the talent and the determination and the luck to escape was Danielle Colliver. She was a damn good executive secretary on the third floor when I took over as Creative Director on the Cadillac account. I had heard rumblings she was not happy with her lot and wanted to talk to me about it.

Danielle wanted to break the chains by becoming a copywriter. I read some of her stuff and agreed to talk to her boss, Pete Moore, Management Supervisor on Cadillac. We worked out an arrangement wherein she would join my creative team on a part-time basis and I would teach her the basics of copywriting. She was a delightful person and we all wanted her to succeed. In the months that followed she did well and soon she was a full-time member of my team.

From copywriter she went to account exec. And then to the client side. She became director of advertising for Chevrolet Division of General Motors Corporation and later headed up the Detroit office of a top-ten agency. It can be done.

How can you break out of the sex trap or avoid it altogether? Blatant militancy is not the answer. Too often, hard-core feminists do their cause more harm than good by finding male chauvinism in every action, every gesture—no matter how innocent.

I was briefing a creative task force of several different teams on the project at hand and used the phrase "you guys and gals". One of the women rose to her feet in anger and protested she was not a gal. Come on. You're trying to make an enemy out of a friend. Ask the women who have worked with me. Ask the women I have helped break out of the trap. Ask Danielle.

One suggestion I have for women in the business is they learn the rules of the game—and play by those rules. As I stated previously, there's always politics. Justice does not always triumph. The most deserving do not always succeed. It helps to know how to play the game. Reread the chapter "THE POLITICS".

But in the end, there is one answer more valid than any other. Excellence. If your performance is consistently better than anybody else's—male of female—you will succeed in the long run. I am sure of it because I have seen it happen too many times not to believe it.

As a creative director, I am interested in one thing above all else in hiring a writer or art director. Will this person help me and my creative team produce great advertising? That's it. Whether this person is male or female, black or white, tall or short, good-looking or ugly doesn't mean a damn.

Excellence and the political smarts to promote that excellence in clever fashion. They will prevail. Use them well.

One last question on the sex trap. Is it fair that you have to work that much harder, be that much better than a male to succeed? Of course not. But such is the nature of the world we live in. Maybe when you rise to a position of power you can help change it.

THE BIGNESS TRAP. When I first joined what is now DMB&B/Bloomfield Hills, it was a large local agency. Then the mergers began. I'm going to spare you the boring details but through the years we became part of a giant agency—the eighth or tenth or twelfth largest in the world, depending upon whom you talk to. DMB&B has over 4,000 employees in offices all over the free world. Maybe more now.

But a few of us who were with MacManus, John & Adams way back when merger mania began have dared to ask a profound question:

So what?

We wondered if we were better off. If our clients were any better served. If the quality of our creative product was enhanced.

We asked the same question many Americans are now posing:

Is bigger necessarily better?

I seriously doubt it.

As a nation, we are beginning to discover that with bigness often comes more structure, more rules, more red tape, more duplication of effort and more inefficiencies. With bigness often comes less individual motivation, less dedication, less esprit de corps.

Most damaging of all, in my opinion, is the added layers of authority that bigness brings...with resulting restrictions on creative freedom.

I am reminded of one of my all-time favorite cartoons published by Y&R a number of years ago. It shows a group of high-level agency execs looking at an ad layout when an agency mailboy happens to walk by. He looks and turns to the CEO with the comment: "Frankly, S.L., I think it stinks."

I love it. I love an organization that is horizontal enough in structure and spirit to listen to everybody.

I have worked for big agencies, small agencies and medium-size shops...as well as on the client side. And now I run my own agency. There are good and bad of all kinds. Size of the agency is not really relevant. What is relevant is the quality of the people in the specific office of that specific agency. Nothing else. "Our 95 offices in 54 countries" isn't going to help you one damn bit to get a superior creative product.

After a lifetime in the advertising business, I am convinced bigness alone isn't worth a poop. Please don't fall into the bigness trap.

THE SECURITY TRAP. This could be the most insidious of all. Ever so slowly through the years, you rise in the ranks and become a real factor in the business. And ever so slowly you begin to compromise your principles and feel less of a reluctance to give in to expediency.

It doesn't have to happen. But so often it does.

When you were young, your battle cry was "Go for Great." Now it seems to be "Don't rock the boat." That's sad. And avoidable.

Nobody has to fall into the Security Trap. I can point to a host of people who have done exceedingly well in this business without becoming its victim.

I've said it before. In the end, you work for yourself in this business. In the end, you are accountable to you.

My wife has a way of looking at this quest for material gain that makes a lot of sense. She maintains that none of us ever really owns anything in this life. We only borrow it for awhile. She's right—isn't she?

Keep going for great. Rock the damn boat. Raise holly hell for what you believe. No matter what.

End of speech. End of chapter.

CHAPTER FIFTEEN

The Gift

"I have been asked what my goal is in life now that I am leaving DMB&B," I said at the gala black-tie party to celebrate my retirement. "It is to become the world's fastest 90-year-old runner."

"And my wife Jil's goal," I continued, " is to make love to the world's fastest 90-year-old runner."

Those are terrific goals and we both hope we can reach them.

But in reality I was thinking more about replacing my days and nights of thinking about advertising with fishing, traveling and taking life easy. And I did. For a month and a half. But do you know what happens when you going fishing every day? Right. It ceases to be fun anymore…at least it did for me.

I had to admit to myself that I missed the business, especially the creative part. Thereupon, I wrote a sales letter for myself and sent it out to every ad agency in Fort Myers. I received one response from the head of an agency that did work for "The Landings", a high-end luxury housing development on the river. He asked me to create a brochure for the place—which I did. It was well received. I got a few bucks for it. And then I got a phone call that was to change my life.

"We've decided DMB&B can no longer handle STI as an account because the billings are too low for us right now," said my old marketing buddy Lu DiSalvo. "Would you be interested in taking it over? They know you well and like your work."

I tried to hide my excitement in responding, "Yeah, I think I would!"

Thus began a storybook client/agency relationship that lasts to this day.

But first I had to form an agency which I called Encore North & South in recognition of the fact that Jil and I are snowbirds with six winter months in Fort Myers and six summer months in a cottage on a beautiful lake in the northeastern part of Michigan. Then I asked Ralph Gardella, a young and talented art director at DMB&B, to join me on a part-time basis (with DMB&B's ok, of course).

It was great to be back in creative but I soon discovered it was a lot tougher than I remembered it at DMB&B. I no longer had a secretary, a staff (other than Ralph) or an agency structure to back me up. But I prevailed and things went well with STI (Safety Technology International, Inc. of Waterford, Michigan). Jack Taylor, founder of the company, and Margie Gobler, his daughter, were excellent people to work with and their business rapidly expanded. Soon, Jack's son, John Taylor, and his other daughter, Lori Taylor, joined the company and STI really took off. Today it is celebrating more than 20 years of helping stop false fire alarms and vandalism around the world with "The Stopper® Line" of more than 50 products.

Soon, I added a few more small accounts but I had to admit I was working way too hard on parts of the business that didn't appeal to me. All those dozens of business things other than my first love…creative.

And then came "the gift". And it came from a most unlikely source—technology.

You see I was the guy who took great pride in the fact that I did all copy work on my trusty old Royal manual typewriter. You know, one of those great big two-tier jobs. I loved banging out my stuff on that baby. It was almost like releasing tensions working out with a punching bag. When DMB&B management gave big IBM electric typewriters to all creative directors, I tried to get used to mine. The trouble was I hit it so hard that from time to time it would skip a space or two. So I gave it back and returned to my Royal manual.

"The gift", as you may have guessed was the computer. It was to change my work life forever.

I owe this transition to Ralph and my son-in-law, Cliff Martin.

At their constant urging I finally purchased a Dell laptop. It was prehistoric by today's standards—with a built-in black-and-white screen and only 40 meg of memory.

Wow! This computer thing was sensational. I could do work faster, easier and better than ever before.

Soon I outgrew the laptop and purchased two tabletop models with printer, monitor, scanner and all the trimming…one for Florida and one for Michigan.

I have now gone through six computer systems and I'm exploring buying my seventh. The computer along with the Internet and all the other toys has truly been a gift from above for me. I'm convinced I would no longer be in the ad biz without it. It would be just too difficult. I can do in a day what used to take me a week…what took a day I can do in an hour, probably less. I'm throwing away most the paper work I had stored in a huge file case and more stuff in the attic. It's all on a couple of CDs.

Ralph and I exchange four-color art for ads and such in minutes through email.

Most important, I can now concentrate on what I love and do best…the creative.

If you're less than 30 years old, you're probably wondering what this old guy is gushing about.

But you have no idea how tough all this was before "the gift."

CHAPTER SIXTEEN

The Decision

Life is all about making decisions—isn't it?

Little almost automatic ones like the blue shirt or the tan…the steak or the fish…go to a movie or stay home and watch TV.

Then there are the biggies. Like who to marry or whether to marry at all…where to go to college…what to make your life's work.

And then there is a decision that can haunt you the rest of your life.

I faced such a decision in California when I worked at Barnes Chase Advertising. Life was good and we were happy—Jil and I. I loved my job as copy/contact (where you're account person, media expert and creative genius all rolled into one). It was a great learning experience and we were doing ok financially.

Then there was a breakup in agency management. Two of the three top guys broke off on their own to form a new agency. The third guy took over as president of Barnes Chase and life went on. Within a few days I received a phone call from the two guys. They wanted to meet with me at a neutral location. I was intrigued and so we met. In brief, they wanted me to join them as the third principal in a new agency in the San Diego area. Its name was to be Lane, Huff & Scott.

"And, of course, we would expect you to bring your accounts with you," they stated. So what was wrong with that? It's done every day in the agency business. Many of the largest and best agencies in the world were started exactly that way.

But it bugged me. Wasn't that a form of stealing? If not that, wasn't it somewhat shady? I agonized over it.

"Lane, Huff & Scott". It had a nice ring to it. Jil and I talked about it. And talked about it. We reasoned this could probably eventually put us on easy street. Plus, both Lane and Huff were much older than I so chances are I would take over full leadership of the agency in a few years. Also, both of them had already been assured of the transfer of major pieces of business. And all they wanted was that I bring along my major account at the time—Non-Linear Systems, Inc. of Del Mar, CA.

There was no doubt in my mind that NLS would agree to come with me.

But I had never gone through mental anguish such as that. I called my brother, Ron Scott, who has since become an ordained minister and with his wife Lenore, also an ordained minister, operates a large Unity Church in Austin, Texas. His advice was to go with my heart.

Finally, I called Mr. Lane, who had previously been president of Barnes Chase, and told him of my soul-searching. "That's ok, Laddybuck, take a little more time." After days of pondering and nights with little sleep, I made my decision.

Then, I sat down with Norm Foster, the new head of Barnes Chase and told him of the tremendous new opportunity facing me. His response was instant. "We'll give you whatever it takes to keep you," he stated. "That includes doubling your salary and giving you a brand new Ford Galaxy station wagon."

I hadn't meant it as a power play. But that was the result.

When I called Mr. Lane to tell him that I decided to stay at Barnes Chase, he said they wanted me to join them even if I decided not to try to bring along NLS. I thanked him for all he has said and done on my behalf but my mind was made up.

I went on to become a senior VP and director at Barnes Chase. Eventually, after seven and a half years in California, Jil and I decided to return to Michigan because we missed our families and other personal reasons.

But it truly has spooked me. Did I make the right decision? What would our lives have been like if I went with Lane, Huff & Scott? What do you think? Was I noble or naïve? Did I do the right thing? I honestly don't know.

This I do know. I never had to worry about hanging my head if I ran across the other 35 people who worked at Barnes Chase at the time. But I still think about it now and then. And wonder.

P.S.

A few years later, I learned that both Lane and Huff had retired and the agency had merged with another.

CHAPTER SEVENTEEN

The KMA

Attorneys call it pro bono work. Advertising people call it a KMA. (As you may know, that's short for Kiss My Ass). Sorry about that but that's what it's called. Probably because it originally was suck-up work done for client's wives, girl-friends or both.

Today the term covers anything that's done free of charge.

Many times it's work done for very worthy organizations—sometimes as part of an agency team and often as not on your own. I'm especially proud of the work I have done for Habitat For Humanity of Lee County in Fort Myers. I started out helping build houses for good people needing a decent place to live. That was fun but I had to give it up because of a heart rhythm problem. (I'm fine now with regular medication.)

To continue to help out I became a member of Habitat's Speakers Bureau. Soon, I was deep into marketing/advertising/PR related projects. It was what I knew best and I honestly think I made a contribution.

That kind of KMA work is fine if it doesn't cut into creating excellent work for your bill-paying clients.

But there is another kind of KMA that can be a problem. That's doing work for amateurs—people who either don't know the business and think they do or people who don't appreciate your work because you're doing it free of charge. Plenty of people still believe what my Dad used to say.

"You get what you pay for." So, if the work is free, how good can it be?

To be honest with you, some of my most unpleasant, frustrating times in this business have been spent working on KMA's. There is, of course, one simple solution. Don't take them on. Learn to say NO!

If your folks brought you up to be a nice person, like me, it is hard to do that...to say no. But for the sake of your sanity, you darn well better learn how.

There can be a great benefit to doing certain kinds of KMA's. That's when they give you an opportunity to learn something new or try something different...to expand your creative abilities. These kind can be good for you...as well as the people you are trying to help. But even then, be wary. Remember your first loyalty is to the people who pay real money for your services.

CHAPTER EIGHTEEN

The Marketing

As chemistry is to the mother science physics, so is advertising to marketing.

We all know this but it's easy to forget...especially if you're a part of a larger organization with specialized departments.

That's one of the beauties of working for a small agency such as Encore North & South. We never forget. The business won't let us. We are forced to look at the big picture all the time. And that's good.

Enter "Dr. T".

When Jil and I first came to Fort Myers after I retired from DMB&B, we both needed some dental work done. And just at that time we received a mailer from one Dr. D. Scott Trettenero. I'm a sucker for advertising and so we called and made an appointment.

"What do you do for a living?" asked Dr. T as he was finishing up some dental repair work for me. He was very interested when I told him what I did and we struck a deal. Advertising/marketing help for dental care. It was the best deal I ever made and I think it has worked out well for him too.

We decided early in the game that I'd call him Scott and he'd call me Scotty. Well, Scott is far more than an excellent dentist. He's also a natural entrepreneur with a real feel for marketing (something not common among dentists).

Through the years, he and I have gone on many marketing adventures together. Some successful…some not. But it has been a tremendous learning experience for me…and I think for him.

One of the most fascinating was called "Creative Endeavors". Meeting in a Fort Myers restaurant one evening, three of us—Scott, Bud Ham (a well-know, Denver-based dental practice consultant) and I—launched a national marketing program for dentists. For a modest fee we would provide everything any private-practice, fee-for-service dentist would need to expand his/her practice through marketing.

To do this, we created two huge binders—one for internal marketing and another covering both internal and external marketing. This was a daring venture because by nature most dentists are unfamiliar with marketing since they receive no schooling on it in dental school. None. Also, there is a feeling shared by many, if not most, health care professionals that marketing is somewhat unethical and beneath them. (With the challenges in today's marketplace, this is changing).

What a task this was! I have the two manuals sitting on the top shelf of my bookcase and I am still impressed by the content—both in quality and quantity.

Our new business did well for a while. But we had made a fatal mistake in our own marketing. We had failed to build in a continuing source of revenue for ourselves. That, and I honestly believe we were several years ahead of our time.

Eventually, we had to discontinue the venture…all three of us sadder but wiser, as they say. But there was, as always, a positive side. It has been said you learn more from your defeats than your victories. And we did. I will never make that mistake again.

A footnote:

Dr. T and I along with another Scott (first name Gary) recently formed a company called Three Scotts, Inc. that shows tremendous promise.

It could pay off big time…or it might turn out to be another great learning experience. Either way, I win.

My message here is to immerse yourself in marketing any way you can. Take added courses in marketing if that's feasible. Most important, think totally in ways to solve your client's problem or meet his business challenge…which may or may not include advertising.

My other message is don't be afraid to take risks. Don't be afraid of failure. As you have just seen, our Creative Endeavors adventure failed despite my long years in the business.

I used to remind the 12 members of my creative team at DMB&B that I never wanted them to be afraid to fail. In fact, I told each of them, he or she had the freedom to fail. I wanted their best work. And fear kills good work.

Please, don't ever settle for safe.

"Behold the turtle," said James Bryant Conant, American chemist. "He makes progress only when he sticks his neck out."

CHAPTER NINETEEN

The Shoot

There is nothing more exciting or more boring than the shoot.

As an ad pro, I have been on all kinds of shoots in all kinds of places—both still shoots for ads, brochures and such as well as Hollywood-style shoots for national TV with well-known celebrities. Sometimes they are magical. Sometimes a pain. All of the time they are hard work for the people doing the actual shooting.

When it came to attending TV shoots, DMB&B had a dumb policy. The creative people (writer and art director) would come up with a great idea…sell it to the client (usually through a creative director such as myself)…and then turn it over to the broadcast department to produce. Often the creative people who came up with the idea wouldn't go to the shoot.

Dumb.

I fought hard to see that I or one or two members of my creative staff would indeed go to the shoot and be working participants in it. But it was a continuing struggle. Fortunately, this is not the policy in most agencies today.

Of all the shoots of one kind or another through all the years, the one I remember best is the one I wasn't a party to at all. Except to sell the result to the Cadillac Advertising Committee. And it wasn't a glamorous TV shoot.

Here is the story.

Fred Simper, one of the all-time great art directors at DMB&B, and I were working together on a national ad for Seville. (I came up with the name Seville just because I liked the sound of it. Research showed it wasn't the top choice in positive response but it had the least negatives going for it. Ed Kennerd, general manager of Cadillac at the time and one of the best in my opinion, said the car will make the name. And he was right.)

Our intended message was to reaffirm the fact that the car was indeed everything Cadillac designed it to be.

To help Fred, I wrote the following copy which appeared exactly this way in the final version of the ad:

A promise kept.

When Seville was first introduced, it was to be a new kind of American luxury car. International in size. Cadillac in craftsmanship. Timeless in styling. Some wondered.

Seville has kept its promise. With subtle refinements to enhance its original concept.

Because of our ongoing quest for perfection, Seville is even more desirable today…

one of the finest production cars built anywhere in the world. Your Cadillac dealer

invites you to experience Seville. It's the only way.

Seville
BY CADILLAC

After considerable discussion, we agreed that a shot over a body of water where we would pick up the reflection of the car might lend a touch of magic to the ad and tie in nicely with our message. Good. But it was February in Detroit.

Fred decided on the San Francisco area, made all the arrangements and headed west.

Now finding a natural setting to meet all our requirements wasn't that simple. In fact, Fred had to hire a crew to literally build a set at a heliport on a strip of land that juts out into the bay that separates San Francisco from Oakland. Finally the pool was dug and filled, the platform constructed at just the right height and covered with gravel. The prepped car, a luxurious copper colored model, was driven into place. And the shoot was on.

Except there was one problem. Not unusual in San Francisco (Oakland, actually), there was a continuing breeze coming in from the Bay which made shooting a water reflection shot almost impossible.

So Fred and the crew got an idea. There was a Greyhound Bus station just across the street so they leased a bus and moved it into place. But that wasn't enough. So they leased a second bus and drove that adjacent to the first one.

Finally, the water was calm enough to get a reflection and the shoot was on again.

But you have to realize two things. First, all this set-building and bus-jockeying had taken time—so much time that nightfall was setting in. In fact, it was almost dark.

Second, the employees at the heliport were breaking up with laughter at the situation. Here were these crazy characters from back east who had to build a pool of water when they were literally surrounded by water.

As a practical joke, one of the pilots decided to take up one of the helicopters and harass these dudes, all in good-natured fun. After taking off, he flew down low over the shoot site and turned on his powerful searchlight.

At just that moment, Fred shouted: "Shoot it!"

When Fred returned to our offices in Bloomfield Hills, Michigan, I was impressed. There were a number of good shots and one great one. That last shot was a beauty. It looks exactly as if it had been taken by moonlight with a gentle breeze creating a reflection arrow pointing at the car.

A week later I reread the copy to the eight members of the Cadillac Advertising Committee and then displayed the shots on a big screen. I showed the five basic reflection shots take by day and early evening with literally no reaction.

Then the moon shot. The response was instant and positive. Even a smattering of applause.

"It was the only shot worth a damn," said Ted Hopkins, the Cadillac assistance general manager.

I took that as a compliment.

As I think back and gaze with renewed admiration at the ad, I ask myself if it was just blind luck. Or untiring hard work. Or both.

"Press on," states the plaque on my wall. "Persistence and determination alone are omnipotent." Or as the man once said: "The harder I work, the luckier I get."

CHAPTER TWENTY

The Toughest Advertising Task

It was certainly the toughest at the time.

Memories of the Detroit race riot were still fresh in the minds of all Americans. And adding to that, Detroit had become the murder capitol of the nation.

It was then officials of the Detroit Visitors and Convention Bureau came to DMB&B to create an advertising campaign to land convention business. Now you have to understand that I was born and raised in Detroit. I still love the place with all its warts. There is so much good about the city and its people. In many ways, I think Detroit has received a bum rap. And continues to suffer that fate.

But when my creative team was assigned the task, I had to face reality.

Getting people to come to Detroit for their convention had to be the toughest advertising task in the world.

Even so, my team and I went to work. And strangely enough, one of our basic marketing planks came from Willie Sutton, perhaps the greatest bank robber of all time.

"So why do you rob banks," they asked Willie.

"That's where the money is," he replied.

And that's one of the most powerful reasons business people should come to Detroit to hold their convention. That's where their customers and prospects are. That's where the money is.

Some of the biggest, best customers for a lot of organizations are head-quarters in the Detroit area or Michigan. General Motors. Ford. Chrysler. Dow Chemical. And many others.

That was plank one.

Plank two. We looked at what our competitors for convention business were already doing in the trade press. They were running beautiful, full color, multi-page ads touting what a great tourist attraction they were. But we were not going to be talking to tourists. And money beats palm trees every time.

Therefore, we decided to "whisper instead of shout"…to tell our prospects in clever, no-nonsense terms that you should come to Detroit if you want bucks instead of a tan. And we would do it with hard-hitting page ads in black and white.

Plank three. Direct mail could be an effective tool for us because there were a relatively small number of key prospects we had to reach. But not just any direct mail. We would send them something they had to look at and keep. We would send them things instead of pieces of paper.

We set firm parameters for these items. Each had to:

1. Tie in dramatically to pay off our message.
2. Be useful or valuable in some way so it wouldn't be thrown away.
3. Be something that could be mailed.
4. Be within our budget.

Our first mailing was so effective, it made the front page of the Detroit newspapers…and local TV. One of the station managers showed our mailer in his editorial and said, "Look what I just received in the mail from the Convention Bureau." And then went on to read every word of our copy. I love those freebies.

We sent a real, live palm tree…with a yellow mailer with green type that read as follows:

The palm tree
vs.
the money tree

If you're dreaming of tropical breezes and swaying palms
for your next convention…our gift should please you.

But if you really want…

A successful convention that's also profitable.

A convention site that's convenient. An hour by air from 60% of the nation's population.

Outstanding and versatile facilities like Cobo Hall or or the magnificent Renaissance Center now under construction.

A labor/management agreement that means smooth setups and efficient service every time.

A prime market that attracts more show traffic and more buyers.

Entertainment, sports events and cultural activities for every taste.

Hotels and restaurants that specialize in friendly service.

Convention specialists ready to assist in every phase of your planning.

Take another look at Detroit

Then, on the back panel of the tri-fold, we carried our call to action…telephone, address, etc.

(The theme—"Take another look at Detroit"—was the suggestion of Chuck Adams, agency president at the time.)

Did this campaign work? You know it did or I wouldn't be talking about it. It was successful beyond our wildest dreams. The one-two punch of the trade press ads and mailers was a smash.

Our second mailing was a cactus with a die-cut mailer saying…

"A pointed reminder that…
some things grow in the sun belt…
…but conventions and trade shows
bloom in Detroit."

Unfortunately, or fortunately—depending upon your point of view—the mailing house didn't wrap the cacti well enough and some dirt/sand fell out of the package when our prospects got the mailing.

We made lemonade out of the lemon by immediately sending out a follow-up letter that said:

"We've been getting the needle because of our cactus mailing.

(Then went on to tell our story again.)

Our third was an orange in the shape of that fruit, saying…

"A tasty reminder that…
…they have the climate for oranges…
…we have the climate for success."

During the following eight years we sent out some wild things but all were on target…including:

A coconut. A set of dice. A presentation pointer. A baseball. Playing cards. Show tickets.

And my all-time personal favorite…a full-size boomerang with the headline **"They keep coming back to Detroit!"**

For seven of the next eight years our campaign was judged Numero Uno in the whole world by the convention pros themselves…the International Society of Convention Professionals. We were second in that other year.

Much of the success of the mailers I credit to a highly talented, dedicated art director on my team named Jim Taliana. We always called him Jim Pix—the counterpart of our copy chief Jim Stano whom we christened Jim Words. Jim Pix loved creating our die-cut mailers for this campaign. And I loved presenting them. In fact, at our annual creative meeting every year, I would place each of our 12 mailer ideas into those little brown paper pages that we used to get at the penny candy store when we were kids. (Yes, there really was candy that cost just a penny.) Then, we would reveal them one at a time until the client selected six. Often, they liked more than six so we'd carry those over into next year. It was a blast.

Well, Jim was in seventh heaven when he was creating new mailers. And then he created his masterpiece.

The headline idea was something like…

If making money is your cup of tea…

Etc. Etc.

Two days later he walked into my office and placed it in front of me. It was beautiful. The whole thing was folded up so that all you could see at first was a charming teacup. Then as you opened it there was an equally lovely teapot behind the cup…with our message. All this was done with only three folds of the paper.

It was extraordinary. Jim told me he worked until 3:30 a.m. to finish it. I believed him.

The amazing thing is that I would show it to other people in my talks at colleges and such, challenging them to duplicate it. None of them could do it, even after I showed them how it was done.

There are all kinds of creativity in advertising.

Even creative folding.

I called him about it just the other day where he is vacationing in Maine with his wife Gloria. He told me his philosophy about the business is that virtually anything is possible. You just have to find out the way to do it. He could be right.

CHAPTER TWENTY-ONE

The Ethics Of The Business
(Sex, booze & other challenges)

You have this long-time, highly profitable client which is one of the finan-cial mainstays of your agency. To top it off, you've just recently been pro-moted to account supervisor and you find yourself aboard a jumbo-jet winging its way to San Francisco for your first big trade show. Beside you in first class is your client counter-part, Mr. Ad Manager.

The two of you seem to hitting if off when he lays this on you.

After claiming that he helped pull the strings to get you promoted (which may or may not be true), he requests that you secure female nightly companionship for him during the length of the show. His tone makes it clear he has sex in mind and he is not kidding.

What is your response? Before you answer I want you to realize you have been married for ten years, have two great kids and just moved into a beautiful new home.

Sadly, in the real world our agency guy made the wrong decision. He did what he was asked. Yes, this did actually happen and I assume in one way or another it's not that uncommon. Back then, when I heard about it, I made up my mind that my answer would have been different than his.

Please understand I am not a religious fanatic or a prude. After two hitches in the Marine Corps as an officer and enlisted man, and encountering all the temptations facing any healthy American male, I have done some things I regret. And even today I have not reached sainthood.

But through the years, I have developed a mini-code of ethics that has served me well. You might find it helpful.

I came into this world with nothing and I'll leave the same way. None of us really owns anything. We just borrow it for a while. That line of thinking puts material things into perspective.

No person or company has enough money to purchase my integrity. If that sounds arrogant, I'm sorry. But it's true. (And it should be true for you also.) I credit this belief to a couple of role models I used to live with—my Dad and Mom.

Please allow me to tell you a short story about Fred and Irene Scott.

Fred was superintendent of a small factory located near downtown Detroit. As such, he received a decent salary that enabled him to support my Mother, two sisters, brother and myself in upper-middle class fashion. Dad's shop was a white oasis in a poor, black neighborhood that today would be called a ghetto.

One day a limo drove up the alley to the shop. A uniformed driver opened the rear door for a distinguished, well-dressed black man. He entered the shop, greeted my Dad and the two shook hands. Then, in the privacy of Dad's office, he made an extraordinary proposal.

This man explained he was a top executive of the numbers racket in Detroit. He said he had knowledge of the winning number next Tuesday. Because of Dad's reputation for integrity in the neighborhood, he felt he could trust him. The man said he would supply a large amount of cash to play the winning number and the two of them would split the profits. Before Dad could reply, he asked him to go home, think about it and give him his answer the following day.

I well recall Mom and Dad discussing this proposal after dinner that night. It was clear the money would have put our whole family on easy street. No more worries about paying for college for us kids, Dad losing his job or unexpected doctor bills. It had to be tempting.

But the discussion was a short one. The answer was an emphatic NO. Neither Mom nor Dad ever talked about the incident again. But I will remember it as long as I live.

As decent human beings, I believe each of us should try to do the right thing solely because of that. It's the right thing to do. I just don't agree that we should live a moral life because of some promised reward after this life. For me, that cheapens it.

When you, representing the agency, and the client disagree on an ad, a TV spot or a piece of copy, I suggest a simple rule to consider. It begins with the fact that you owe it to the client to explain exactly why the agency rationale for what it did and how it will benefit the client. Let's say the client still disagrees. Ok, I look at it this way—it's the client's nickel. So if it isn't illegal or immoral, I go ahead and do it the client's way.

Of course, I won't put that ad or spot in my portfolio. And, if the disagreements continue, you should consider whether the business is worth the hassle. But short-term, think about Scott's rule.

Now, about the booze problem. (By the way, never use that word if you are pitching a liquor account. The good folks at Hiram-Walker across the river in Windsor told us that.)

Alcohol can be a special challenge in ad biz because it so readily available. If you're an art director, "suit" (account person) or member of the agency's media or broadcast departments, someone is always ready to take you to lunch. And, of course, you have to have a drink or two to loosen up. It can be great fun. I've spent many a pleasant afternoon with good food, good drink and good company.

It can also be deadly.

When I took over as creative director on the Cadillac account at DMB&B, I inherited an excellent, experienced art supervisor. But I soon discovered I had to do all my business with him in the morning. The rest of the day he was either absent or crocked. I tried talking to him but that had no effect. So I went to the account supervisor.

"We have a problem," said I in explaining the situation. No explanation on my part was really necessary because he had known about it for years. Time and again, he and other third-floor residents had seen him staggering down the walkway from the parking lot to the front door.

"No, George, you have a problem," he replied. It was the classic agency cop-out.

I thought about it, made a decision and went to Ron Monchak, the head of the creative department and my boss. I told him I had respect for the guy who had been with the agency for almost 20 years, but our creative team couldn't live with this. I recommended we demote the guy, transfer him to another group and get him professional help. Ron agreed.

You cannot believe the bitterness when I told him. He didn't speak to me for years. But I am convinced I may well have saved his life. Years later he told me that.

Please, allow me to state the obvious. Be careful. I have seen many brilliant careers destroyed by booze. Don't let it happen to you.

Now about some of those other challenges.

Please don't play the "Phony Game." .Don't load your briefcase up with magazines and other junk so it looks like you're taking work home. You're not really fooling anyone.

. Don't stay late at the office when you don't have to. So many people do this in some agencies that it's almost expected. If you've given your job your best from 9 to 5, you're going to be totally beat. So you're not going to be very creative anyway. Of course, there are exceptions when you and your team have to work late but it should be only for a real emergency.

. Don't take credit for somebody else's work. And, if someone pulls this crap on you, don't let them get away with it. It amazes me how often this happens. Damn it. It's stealing. If you let people get away with it, they will think you're a wimp. And you don't want that.

I have always believed it's far better to be respected than loved. With people who really count and turn out to be true friends, you will be both.

I feel a little uncomfortable talking about agency ethics but it can be important to your career. After all these years, I have come to a very simple conclusion. Doing the right thing is just so much easier long-term than the alternative. Every time I have veered off that path I have lived to regret it.

Life is too short and too precious to make needless enemies, worry about somebody discovering your dirty little secret or spending your days looking over your shoulder.

CHAPTER TWENTY-TWO

The Simple Truth

Someday, if you are fortunate enough to live as long as I have, you will look back at your stuff and make a judgment. You will decide the material you have produced has merit...or it does not.

Of course, you are—I am—prejudiced. But by now you are a damn good editor who can separate the winners from the also-rans. When you go through your work, you will make three piles.

Pedestrian.   *Good.*   *Outstanding.*

Don't fight it. Make your decisions quickly...by gut feel. As a disinterested consumer might.

There. We're done. How do the piles stack up? Okay, it's a good feeling to know you've created some things with real merit. Now take a closer look at that outstanding pile. In doing so, you will perceive a profound truism of this business.

GREAT ADVERTISING IS SIMPLE.

But, creating great advertising that is simple yet innovative...direct yet involving...is anything but simple. It is the supreme challenge facing the creative person. As I look closely at the stuff that pleases me, I am struck anew by the power and the sheer beauty of simplicity presented with conviction and believability. Each ad, each commercial that makes my outstanding pile uses a solution that now seems obvious. At the time it was anything but.

I believe part of the trouble we ad folks have is getting too close to the problem. I'm sure of it. We forget consumers have no basic interest in what we have to say. More than that, they are conditioned to ignore advertising. So how can we hope to reach any consumer with any message unless we make it worth his or her while? One false note...one stray path...and we've lost him or her forever.

No doubt you're heard it before but please remember KISS. Keep It Simple, Stupid.

I must confess to you I haven't always followed the brilliant (and obvious) advice I present to you now. As difficult as the creative challenge is, we often do all we can to make it more difficult. We over-analyze it. Over-think it. Over-work it. When that happens, we can over-look the solution even though it's there in front of us. I know I've done it.

Further, we subject ourselves to any number of impossible rules and standards. "Every great ad must do these 12 things!" Or seven. Or 20. Of course, these guidelines can be useful enough to check out the completed creative work. But if you fill your head with all this stuff before the fact, you are doomed.

I'm reminded of the story of why Einstein couldn't or wouldn't drive a car. As he sat behind the wheel, all he could think of was the thousands of different things that were happening under the hood once the key was turned. It was too much to ponder all that and drive too.

Most of us ordinary humans can only do one thing at one time—if we hope to do it well. We have to keep it simple.

We have to start with the basics—who, what and why. Who (or whom) are we trying to reach?

What are we trying to sell in human terms (security, prestige, peace of mind, etc.)? And why should anybody buy it—or this brand versus another?

Once we answer these questions, we can proceed to the more complex. One step at a time.

Simple. Simple. Simple.

There seems to be a conspiracy to complicate our lives in every which way. Sometimes, it's downright silly. Example: Three times last night I saw one of Scott's Golden Rules of Simplicity violated for no reason. The TV spot ends with a theme-line or call to action supered on the screen but the voice-over says something completely different.

Result: The consumer ignores the punch line. Dumb. How much simpler, easier and more effective to have the voice-over say exactly what appears on the screen.

The secret to great advertising?

It's simple.

CHAPTER TWENTY-THREE

The Q&A

One of the things I enjoy most about giving talks on advertising before any kind of group is the question and answer session that follows. Here are some questions I'd want to ask me if I were you.

Q: What's the best way to latch on to a job at a big-time agency?

A: *Start out at a good medium to small-sized agency and learn your craft. You'll learn more and do it faster and better while getting a feel for what phase of the business you want to specialize in. Also, it makes getting a job at a big-time agency that much easier because you have something to show off your abilities.*

Q: Would you want your son or daughter to go into advertising?

A: *Most certainly, if he or she had the talent and the desire.*

Q: What was the most difficult part of your job?

A: *Telling the truth to wonderful, young people who wanted to be copywriters but didn't have the basic talent. I tried to do this as tactfully as possible but I felt I wasn't doing them any favor to lie to them. There are plenty of other good jobs in this business and I would remind them of that fact.*

Q: How do you know when an ad is creative?

A: *Not by winning awards. An ad is creative when it works. Period.*

Q: I gather you don't like awards.

A: *Only when I win.*

Q: Are you serious?

A: *I've won my share of them but in my heart of hearts, I don't put much stock in them. There are too many cases of an agency winning an award for a client and then losing the business. Also, I have served as a judge for many ad competitions along with other people who were far less qualified than me. Our opinions often varied widely and I seldom felt confident the best (most successful) work was victorious.*

Q: How can you know whether you can be a successful creative person?

A: *Only by doing it. I've always said a singer sings, a painter paints and a writer writes. The same holds true for an art director. He or she practices his/her craft. It is not just something to do to make money. It is who and what you are.*

Q: What part of the business do you like best?

A: *It's a toss-up between presenting and writing sales letters. It might seem strange but I love to write a sales letter. I love the challenge of getting inside the heads of the people we are trying to reach and then grabbing them. getting them involved in our message and motivating them through their own self-interest.*

Q: What's the secret of good advertising?

A: *What I just said. The only way you can get anybody to do anything is to motivate him or her through their own self-interest. That sounds simple but you see it violated everywhere you look. That's why really good advertising still stands out...still works. And always will as the trends come and go.*

Q: Which is your all-time least favorite ad or TV commercial?

A: *The 'ring around the collar" spot a few years ago. I hate it. But I remember it was for Wisk detergent so by my definition it must have been creative. And it must have been successful because it ran a lot of years. But I still hated it and never used Wisk. But then I never did the laundry in our family either.*

Q: Of all the theme lines you've come up with through the years, which one do you like best?

A: *Probably the one I did for Kirsch Drapery Hardware, Mini-Blinds and such... "We do windows".*

Q: What's the best part of this business?

A: *The people.*

Q: What's the worst part of this business?

A: *The people.*

Q: What was your biggest thrill in advertising?

A: *Winning the DMB&B/Bloomfield Hills "Ad of the Year" award in 1982. It was for my Cadillac TV commercial entitled "Just for you". I received a handsome plague, plenty of cash and a week aboard the agency yacht touring the Caribbean with my wife Jil and a crew of two. It was great.*

Q: Would you do it all over again, if you had the chance?

A: *Only if I had a computer.*

So long and God bless you.

The Last Word

If you're less than 40 years old, you're probably not going to believe this. But it is true. Life is finite. Your advertising career has a beginning, middle and end. Knowing this, you have to decide what you want most out of the advertising business. Fame. Fortune. Or both. May I suggest there is something more valuable and long-lasting than mere material gain—as cornball as this may sound. The word is fun. After 35 years and more in it, I believe you can have more fun in this business than almost any other. With the possible exception of show biz. For God's sake enjoy it. Live it up. Drink it in. Do your best. Be true to you. Have fun.

Without selling your soul.

About the Author

His more than 35 years in advertising has resulted in hundreds of millions of dollars in sales of everything from Cadillacs to cheese from drapery hardware to computer software from dental care to psychiatric care...from paints to plastics...from newspapers to fishing lures and just about everything else in between. Dozens of successful agency creative people who worked for and with him sing his praises...as do hundreds of students who attended his classes...and hundreds more executives of the clients he has served.

After 21 years as creative director at D'Arcy Masius Benton & Bowles in Bloomfield Hills, MI, George A. Scott retired as a senior vice president in 1986 and promptly founded his own creative communications business called Encore North & South with offices in Florida and Michigan. He is also a founding partner of Creative Endeavors, a national marketing organization for dentists committed to excellence and a founding partner of Three Scotts, Inc., a company to market unique dental supplies.

At DMB&B, he headed a 12-person team of writers and art directors to create print, broadcast and collateral advertising for Cadillac, Kirsch, General Tire, The Detroit Free Press, Bendix and a wide range of other accounts. He was also founder and chancellor of "Brown Bag U.", an organization to teach the basics of the advertising business to younger members of the agency in DMB&B offices across the U.S.

Since retiring from DMB&B, he has taught two terms of advertising copywriting at Wayne State University. Earlier, he taught marketing at San Diego State U. Prior to DMB&B, he served as a vice president and director for Barnes Chase Advertising in San Diego, an advertising staff member for The Dow Chemical Company in Midland, MI, and a reporter and sports editor for The Marion Star in Marion, Ohio where he wrote daily sports columns called "Out On The Limb" and "Scott's Sportscope". He also served two hitches in the U.S. Marine Corps and rose to the rank of first lieutenant.

He has received dozens of awards and honors for both his creative work and his contributions to marketing education. These include "DMB&B Ad of the Year" in 1982, the "Aid To Advertising Education Award" from the American Advertising Federation and two gold and seven silver "Caddies" for creative excellence from the Creative Advertising Club of Detroit. His ad entitled "Last of a Magnificent Breed" was selected as one of the 100 greatest automotive advertisements of all time. He was also the first person outside of the Michigan Consolidated Gas Company to receive the prestigious MichCon Award for Marketing Achievement. An avid sports fan, Scott has run nine marathons. He has also written and published several books of poetry. He and his wife, Jil Audrey Scott, share their time between a home in Ft. Myers, Florida and a cottage on Rifle Lake, south of Mio, Michigan.

www.ingramcontent.com/pod-product-compliance
Lightning Source LLC
Chambersburg PA
CBHW030819180526
45163CB00003B/1351